Divide and School

Divide and School:
Gender and Class Dynamics in Comprehensive Education

John Abraham

 The Falmer Press

(A member of the Taylor & Francis Group)
London • Washington, D.C.

UK   The Falmer Press, 4 John Street, London WC1N 2ET
USA   The Falmer Press, Taylor & Francis Inc., 1900 Frost Road, Suite 101, Bristol, PA 19007

First published in 1995

A catalogue record for this book is available from the British Library

Library of Congress Cataloging-in-Publication Data are available on request

ISBN 0 7507 0390 3 cased
ISBN 0 7507 0391 1 paper

Jacket design by Caroline Archer

Typeset in 10½/12pt Bembo by
Graphicraft Typesetters Ltd., Hong Kong.

Printed in Great Britain by Burgess Science Press, Basingstoke on paper which has a specified pH value on final paper manufacture of not less than 7.5 and is therefore 'acid free'.

This book is dedicated to Linda Creasey

Contents

Contents

Acknowledgments

I am extremely grateful to all the teachers and pupils in the school who participated in the research, and especially to one of the deputy headteachers for his cooperation beyond the line of duty. Many people have encouraged me during the preparation of this book. These include Colin Lacey, Lin Creasey, Barry Cooper, Bill Poole and Malcolm Clarkson. Thanks are also due to Jackie Day for ensuring a smooth pathway to publication.

Introduction

This book is concerned with class and gender divisions in secondary education, with particular emphasis on comprehensive schooling. Most of the book reports on empirical research carried out during 1986 in a comprehensive school which will be known as Greenfield Comprehensive. I examine how social class and gender divisions occurred within the comprehensive school despite the egalitarian goals sometimes attributed to comprehensivization. The research shows that the comprehensive school is not necessarily one which challenges dominant social class and gender divisions to any significant degree. Indeed, to some extent it can serve to reproduce them.

The book is critical of comprehensive schooling, but it is not an exercise in 'school bashing' or 'teacher bashing'. I do not believe that Greenfield was a 'bad' school either in its performance or treatment of pupils. In some ways it was progressive and the staff afforded me good cooperation and hospitality. I did not find any teachers who deliberately attempted to discriminate against pupils on the grounds of social class or gender. Schools are very complex social systems and often teachers are as much victims and products of that system as they are upholders of it, for better or worse. Furthermore, I do not claim to give an exhaustive account of the school. No doubt there are many positive aspects of the school left unmentioned.

Rather, the purpose of the book is to contribute to a process of cumulative understanding about the internal social workings of the comprehensive school. Through this collective understanding we can move forward to propose and perhaps implement informed changes. As I have discussed elsewhere, that task cannot be intelligibly achieved by adopting a position of social indifference or value neutrality (Abraham 1994). This is because people always have some reasons for pursuing knowledge and those reasons are inevitably connected to some values, albeit sometimes implicitly and unconsciously. The explicit realization of this feature of social science has led to a great fuss about the need for reflexivity in sociological research.

By reflexivity is meant researchers asking of themselves the sort of questions they pose about their research subjects. For example, a reflexive sociologist of education wishing to discover the values underpinning a group of deviant pupils would also ask what values underpin his or her own research project. The principle of reflexivity is inescapable in the social sciences because their enquiries can always be turned back on themselves. In principle, there can always be a 'sociology of sociology of education', for instance.

A great deal of feminist research prides itself on applying the principle of reflexivity (Williams, 1993), which Riddell defines as:

> making explicit [her] political and theoretical positions and their impact on the process of data collection. (Riddell, 1992, p. 17)

Yet Riddell rarely expands on her political position, beyond reiterating that she is a feminist, not to mention explicating its impact on data collection. We may note that her declaration that she is a feminist is minimally informative because as feminists, such as Gelsthorpe (1992) and Williams (1993) have emphasized, there is great diversity within feminism and feminist methodology.

Other commentators outside the feminist camp have had fun playing with the notion of reflexivity. This involves such antics as authors having conversations with themselves in the text about why they wrote their previous sentence (Woolgar, 1988). What those contributions illustrate is that reflexivity taken to its extreme can produce work that tells us a great deal about the authors' thinking behind trivial matters of sentence construction, but very little about research subjects. By contrast, Riddell has something socially significant to say about schooling, gender and the curriculum. Understandably, therefore, she discusses primarily her research subjects and results rather than herself, though this is not to ignore the fact that the social scientist is always part of the research situation.

This brief excursion into social scientists' treatment of reflexivity demonstrates that, in practice, authors have to make a judgment about the extent of reflexivity that is desirable in their writings. It is not simply a matter of 'the more reflexivity the better', as some sociologists seem to imply. I prefer to adopt a position of constrained reflexivity, which outlines the basic values and principles underlying the research, but avoids continual reference to self-motivation. The two basic principles guiding the research in this book are: that it is socially and, therefore, educationally desirable to reduce social class and gender divisions and inequalities; and that the education system should be interventionist, not neutral about class and gender inequality.

An inspection of class and gender divisions in schooling is timely because over the last fifteen years substantial changes in the British occupational structure have occurred. Against a backdrop of rising unemployment there has been a growth in flexible, part-time work in the service sector and a decline in traditional manual jobs. This has been paralleled by growing male unemployment, especially amongst low-skilled men with poor educational qualifications, and by a significant increase in women's participation in the labour market and education (Lees, 1993; Payne and Payne, 1994). Such changes have led to debates in sociology and social policy about whether class and gender relations are undergoing fundamental transformations, including the development of an 'underclass' in association with a 'middle-mass classlessness' and a redistribution of domestic labour from women to men (Crompton and Sanderson, 1990; Field, 1989; Gregson and Lowe, 1994; Mann, 1992; Riddell, 1992; Saunders, 1990; Westergaard, 1992; Wheelock, 1990). It is beyond the scope of this book to attempt to settle these debates, but they do underline the importance of considering what role secondary schooling plays in preparing young people for this potentially dynamic social terrain.

I examine social-class and gender divisions within the school mainly in terms of organization, deviance, pupil subcultures, school knowledge, and teacher ideology. The research takes an ethnographic approach, but is not confined to quantitative or qualitative methods; both are applied according to the nature of the research questions asked and the data collected. Moreover, the ethnographic approach taken does not imply that the research eschews hypothesis-testing; exploratory and hypothesis-testing methods are utilized depending on the demands of the research enquiry.

The opening chapter introduces the reader to certain aspects of the debate about comprehensive education and provides some social and historical context for the case-study which follows. Chapter 2 critically reviews the main developments in the sociology of education that are related to social class and gender, with a view to providing a firm theoretical foundation for the research methodology, which is outlined in Chapter 3.

In Chapter 4 I consider how inter- and intra-set differentiation can reproduce and create social-class-based divisions amongst the pupil population. Teachers' use of an 'ability' ideology to stereotype pupils according to their position within the setting hierarchy is also discussed. This is particularly important in understanding social-class divisions within the comprehensive in view of the fact that most working-class pupils are at the bottom of the hierarchy and most pupils at the top are middle-class. Chapter 5 explores how gender differentiation manifests itself within the school and examines some of the gender characteristics within the subcultures of anti-school boys and girls. In particular, some of these characteristics account for the pupils' hostility to the school — a point which is often neglected in studies of sex differences which concentrate on performance and certification.

In Chapter 6 the focus shifts to the organization of school knowledge. I examine how the comprehensive school can act as a site of social reproduction via the subject-option process. Particular attention is paid to the pupils' own accounts of this process and how they are involved in it. The next chapter takes a more detailed look at the differentiation of school knowledge by focusing on the gendering and stratification of the mathematics, English and French curricula. Insofar as stratification is based on social-class divisions, it has differential effects on pupils of different social-class groups. This is, of course, related to the organizational differentiation discussed in Chapter 4. In fact, all the chapters on the school intertwine in various ways as one would expect since they all bear on the same real experiences.

Chapter 8 considers how the teachers' general ideology about sex roles and sexism might be related to their use and choice of curriculum materials. This chapter also reveals that there are considerable differences between the gender value systems of the teachers themselves, and that very considerable changes in the perspectives of some teachers would be required before they could embrace a policy for anti-sexist pedagogy. Finally, in the closing chapter I draw out the main conclusions of the research and, in the light of recent government policies on secondary schooling, I return to some of the political issues broached in Chapter 1.

Chapter 1

Comprehensive Education: Past Debates and Future Ideals

In Britain over the last few decades there has been no shortage of debate and dispute over the desirability of comprehensive secondary schools. Secondary schooling remains a burning issue and continues to have a high political profile, sometimes taking the centre stage in general elections. Tracking the debate on comprehensive education is rather like stalking an intellectual chameleon. The debate often changes direction with subtle changes in definitions and meanings. There are difficulties, therefore, in defining *the* comprehensive debate. Nevertheless, since this book is an empirical study of a comprehensive school, I think it is valuable to identify some of the main points of contention regarding comprehensivization.

By the mid-1960s the Labour Party was won over to the idea of comprehensive schools and in 1965 the Labour Government announced plans for widespread comprehensivization. The oft-cited Department of Education and Science Circular 10/65 may be regarded as the first *explicit* attempt by a British Government to define the possible forms that comprehensive reorganization might take. However, as Ball (1981) points out, that document did not set out any positive aims for comprehensive schooling. In addition the Government failed to define any educational goals for pupils *within* the comprehensive schools. Consequently, a considerable variation in philosophies for comprehensive education has developed and so too have different types of comprehensives.

Aims and Principles

Despite government reticence, McPherson and Willms (1987) believe that it is possible to define six purposes of the comprehensivization reforms, as follows:

1 no selection of pupils at secondary level;
2 the establishment of one type of secondary school — the all-through fixed catchment comprehensive;
3 compulsory schooling should not end before the first stage of public certification;

4   the reduction in between-school variation in pupils' backgrounds
    so that the school should represent a 'fuller cross-section' of the
    community;
5   the elimination of the 'creaming' of 'able' pupils from one school
    catchment to another; and
6   increased access to certification.

The proposal that comprehensive schools should represent a fuller
cross-section of the community entirely neglected, of course, the 7 per
cent of elite pupils who attend private schools. Leaving this detail aside,
it can be seen that none of these 'purposes' says anything explicit about
ideals for education as such. Rather they are prescriptions for certain organizational arrangements. Insofar as we can infer the educational principles underlying these purposes then we can regard them as being bounded
by either the 'meritocratic' or the 'integrative' models of comprehensive
education (Ball, 1981). For example, (1), (3) and (6) can be regarded as
concerned with equality of opportunity and the maximization of pupils'
qualifications whatever the consequences for social relationships (the
meritocratic principle). On the other hand, (2), (4) and (5) represent concerns based on the idea that all children, despite social background, should
attend the same secondary school with the aim of increasing social solidarity (the integrative principle). None of these six purposes can be readily
related to the egalitarian principle which distinguishes between equality
and equality of opportunity. The egalitarian view aims to reduce inequality. It maintains that changes in the educational process such as the development of cooperative learning and greater openness between the school
and community are required to achieve the goal of equality.

The Threat to Competitiveness

By 1970 support at least for the meritocratic and integrative principles of
the comprehensive idea had grown within the Conservative Party. However, with the election of three successive Thatcher Governments from
1979 the new political Right were in the ascendancy. Cross-party consensus on comprehensive schooling was broken as the new Right began its
offensive against comprehensive ideals, reaching a peak in the mid-1980s.
The Right criticized comprehensive schools for being too egalitarian and
accused them of contributing to Britain's poor competitive economic
performance despite the fact that egalitarianism was precisely the definitional
component of comprehensives which had been lacking. The jungle of
ideological and causal connections which emerged in the comprehensive
debate was well illustrated in 1986 when a headteacher did not allow
competitive sports during the school Sports Day, and when the Inner
London Education Authority's physical education inspector declared that

competitive team sports should not be played during school hours. These events prompted Norman Tebbit, then Conservative Party Chairman, to defend competitive sports in schools and to retort: 'Can you imagine that our Japanese or German competitors in the business world are poisoning the minds of their youngsters in such a way?' (Anon, 1986a). Another commentator sought to defend competitiveness within comprehensive schools on the grounds that the 'transition' from tribal to industrialized societies involved competition. (Sofer, 1986).

In the early comprehensives the practice of rigid streaming (by forms) of pupils according to 'ability' tests was common. By the late 1960s that practice was being criticized for re-creating, in effect, the old selective system within the same school. Moreover, one study found that in a situation of rigid streaming there was 'no evidence that comprehensive education contributed[d] to the breaking down of the barriers of social class which divide adults and children alike' (Ford, 1969, pp. 129–30). Consequently, during the late 1970s some comprehensives began de-streaming by experimenting with 'mixed ability' classes. This too came under attack by the political Right in the 1980s. Linking 'the national interest' with education policy Kenneth Baker, the Secretary for Education, condemned 'mixed ability' classes:

> The ultimate goal of socialist education is the mixed-ability choir where the flat, the toneless and the stone deaf all make their contribution to cacophony — and all this has to be compulsorily applauded. The trouble with our nation is that not enough encouragement is given to excellence or competition. (Anon, 1986b)

He located the philosophy of state schools, including comprehensives, firmly within the meritocratic model by stating that 'equality of opportunity means the achievers must be allowed to achieve' (Anon, 1986c).

On a similar note Chris Patten, the Education Minister, argued that pupils should be grouped and banded according to their abilities and aptitudes with the justification that 'you cannot treat them [children] alike if you want to be fair to each one of them' (Anon, 1986d). That view also found support outside the Conservative Government. Stevens (1980) declared that postponing streaming in comprehensives could not be defended if it put 'bright' pupils in comprehensives at a disadvantage when competing for university places.

In these comments we find comprehensive education accused of fostering non-competitiveness and failing to give the meritocratic principle of equality of opportunity sufficient priority over other ideals. Intertwined with this is the implication that comprehensive education hampers the pursuit of 'excellence' and the progress of the 'most able' children. Ideals for education are readily mixed with national economic aspirations, presuppositions about the performance of comprehensive schools and even crude theories of industrialization.

Principles and Performance Indicators

Some academic researchers have brought much more order to the discussion by concentrating on the historical record of comprehensive schools in terms of 'output', though they have done so at the expense of the question of ideals for comprehensive education. In 1983 the results of three such 'output' studies were published. Marks, Cox and Pomian-Srzadnicki (1983) maintained that their research showed that a fully selective secondary-schooling system led to substantially higher 'O'-level, CSE and 'A'-level examination results than a fully comprehensive system. By contrast, Gray, McPherson and Raffe (1983) concluded that comprehensives seemed to have raised average attainment and Steedman (1983) suggested that overall trends in examination results could not be explained by going comprehensive. Reviews of these studies have pointed to some serious problems with the research carried out by Marks *et al.* (1983) in terms of the appropriateness of the research design with respect to the conclusions drawn (Fogelman, 1984; Clifford and Heath, 1984). Thus, systematic research so far carried out on output performance seems to offer little support to the criticisms of comprehensives put forward by the political Right.

One problem with the output-performance controversy is that it may lead to a neglect of more fundamental questions concerning the educational practice and principles of comprehensive schooling. For example, Heath (1984), writing 'in defence of comprehensive schools', comments that they have been criticized by the political Left 'for failing to lead us to the promised land of equality of opportunity'. Here we see that the ideal for comprehensive education that is being defended is narrowly located within the meritocratic principle. The integrative and egalitarian ideals are not even considered. Despite this the integrative and egalitarian principles have to some extent been rescued by David Hargreaves (1982) and Reynolds, Sullivan and Murgatroyd (1987).

Hargreaves (1982) is particularly concerned that schools should confer on pupils 'a genuine sense of dignity' which would form the basis for a 'stronger national solidarity' and the ability to resolve conflicts between subcommunities. In rejecting meritocratic concerns he suggests that all 16-plus examinations should be abolished and that from the age of 11 to 15 pupils should follow a core curriculum which is sensitive to the needs of the community, and one which acknowledges current social-class inequalities with respect to schooling. Hargreaves acknowledges that his proposals might lead to a decline in the academic attainment of 'gifted' pupils, but argues that the improvement in their general education would more than compensate for this. He proposes that half of the curriculum, the common core, should be organized in terms of mixed-ability groups but concedes that 'much of the academic option work would almost certainly have to be streamed or set by ability if most pupils are to be stretched'.

As for Reynolds *et al.* (1987), their vision of a comprehensive is a school which is much more collectively organized, and which exhibits distribution of power among a greater number of people involved in the educational system. They recommend that the 'deep structure' of relationships and feelings in comprehensives must be the focus for reform rather than merely concerns about resources. Like Hargreaves they accept that the ideal comprehensive should not impose an entirely universal curriculum on pupils ('the egalitarian steampress model'), but favour some universalistic elements combined with some selectivistic differentiated curricula as well. The differentiation would be based upon the different 'abilities' of the pupils which they claim define different 'needs'.

Ability, Needs and Naturalization

Even the much more detailed contributions on the educational nature of comprehensives by Hargreaves and Reynolds *et al.*, leave a few grey areas in need of clarification. For example, what sort of 'ability' is it that defines pupils' needs? It is not adequate merely to imply that 'giftedness' defines a pupil's needs because needs have to be related to some goals in order to make any sense. There is also the question of what sort of 'giftedness' is valued in the educational system. Some pupils might be very 'gifted' at helping others who have difficulty in achieving particular goals yet those 'gifted' pupils are likely to be separated from those they could help in a system divided by ability hierarchies. Helping others could be more of a need than striving ahead competitively for at least some pupils. An education which emphasizes cooperative learning and genuine caring for other people is likely to nurture in pupils different needs to those that would develop under a pressured environment dominated by competitive certification. This is not to suggest that individuals have the same abilities to perform certain specified tasks, but before we accept and systematize some hierarchy of ability we should be much clearer about the criteria for judging ability in the first place. Furthermore, education is stripped of any social purpose if it is assumed that abilities define needs. Needs may be much better defined according to desires to live in a certain kind of society, as David Hargreaves (1982) appreciates. Thus, needs are politically contestable. For example, someone might be *able* to be trained as an astronaut, but whether training to be an astronaut is a *need* must surely be a different question.

It follows that to claim that pupils will have different needs on the basis of their different abilities must be assuming some underlying model of pupil and societal development. Unfortunately, such a model never really emerges in the writings of those who advocate differentiated schooling based on ability hierarchies. Reynolds *et al.* (1987) say that 'the low ability child also may need a slightly different curriculum' but they do not explain why this is a need except by some implicit reference to standards within the curriculum. Nor are we told how low ability is determined and in relation to what broader social purposes for education. The result is a naturalization of ability hierarchies which runs the risk of being applied as a rationale for social inequality (Shilling, 1992).

Sex, Gender and Naturalization

The comprehensive debate has been largely concerned with meritocracy, integration and egalitarianism for social classes. As the momentum to challenge class divisions in secondary schools grew in official circles during the 1960s, matters of gender divisions and sexual inequality were neglected. In 1963 the Newsom Report naturalized the common social situation of women in Britain as a justification for an education dedicated to maintaining gender divisions:

> We try to educate girls into becoming imitation men and as a result we are wasting and frustrating their qualities of womanhood at great expense to the community . . . In addition to their needs as individuals our girls should be educated in terms of their main social function which is to make for themselves, their children and their husbands a secure and comfortable home and to be mothers. (cited in Lees, 1993, p. 154)

Coupled with such neglect of sexual inequality, comprehensivization increased the number of co-educational secondary schools, as single-sex grammar schools merged into new comprehensives taking boys and girls under the same roof. The major concern that has linked the comprehensive debate with gender issues is the feminist argument that comprehensive education has accentuated the academic failure of girls relative to boys. This has been raised by Shaw (1980), whose main points deserve considerable attention.

She claims that the pressure to discontinue all-female colleges and single-sex schools had the same ideological basis as attempts to exclude women from education in a previous era, namely a defensive response to the threat that women might take over certain advantages reserved for men. Secondly, Shaw contends that the consequence of integrating boys and girls in co-education comprehensives was that girls received a poorer education in order to allow traditional sex roles to flourish in a 'boy–girl' environment. In particular, she notes that pupils who opted for science subjects at secondary school were more likely to remain in formal education, and that girls who were in single-sex schools were more likely to choose science subjects than their sisters in comprehensives. According to Shaw, therefore, comprehensivization increased differentiation and segregation between boys and girls.

On this argument the integrative principle of comprehensive education is dysfunctional along sex lines and serves to disguise conflicts of interest between boys and girls. That conflict, it is proposed, manifests itself by girls being turned into a 'negative reference group' for boys. As Shaw explains:

> In a competitive and selective educational system such as our own, being better than someone else is of vital importance if children are to believe their success. They have to be able to recognize themselves in the processes of selection and examination, and they do this by being able to identify those who are not as successful. As a group, boys have an advantage over girls simply because their success is more public. (Shaw 1980: 71–72)

Finally, Shaw is confident that schools run by women for women can provide a model of educational excellence that should not be undermined by comprehensivization.

One crucial issue is whether comprehensive ideals should be abandoned because some practices of comprehensivization have short-changed girls relative to boys. Proponents of the egalitarian comprehensive ideal should support uncompromisingly the elimination of sexism and gender inequality in mixed comprehensive schools. Here I am in agreement with Shaw, but rather than responding to sexual inequality in comprehensives by 'ghettoizing' pupils into single-sex schools, substantial efforts need to be made to change comprehensives into institutions which are strongly opposed to such inequality, whatever its source.

At the risk of seeming overly idealistic, I would suggest that Shaw is far too accepting of the competitiveness and selective nature of secondary schooling. If boys achieve at the expense of girls because of competitive use of 'negative reference groups', then the fundamental challenge for the comprehensive is to alter the framework of achievement. The argument for single-sex schooling shies away from confronting that challenge, even though it may produce more highly competitive and successful women. Shaw does not consider the possibility that such a model of excellence *may* be undesirable for either boys or girls. Besides, as with ability hierarchies, judgments about the quality of what boys or girls achieve (such as 'excellence') depend on broader social purposes for education. It is not obvious that the sexual make-up of the school should form part of that quality judgment.

A second major limitation of Shaw's critique of comprehensivization is that it is insufficiently discriminating to take account of gender differences

7

between members of the same sex. Girls and boys are treated as uniform blocks with undifferentiated interests. This puts too much emphasis on sex differences and not enough on differences in gender orientation. Trenchard (1988), for example, discusses how young lesbians at school were subjected to heterosexist harassment from other girls as well as boys. An overly narrow emphasis on sex differences runs the risk of naturalizing all gender divisions as boy–girl divisions, especially in the context of proposals for single-sex schooling. Nevertheless, Shaw's position is an important intervention in a comprehensive debate which has otherwise paid far too little attention to gender division and inequalities.

Conclusion

Concepts such as 'ability', 'need' and 'equality of opportunity' should not be adopted uncritically and cannot be discussed in a social and political vacuum. Too often socially established hierarchies of 'ability' are naturalized and then fed into the meritocratic equation as fixed entities instead of being deconstructed. Social-class and gender differences have been, and continue to be, prime targets for such naturalization, which helps to justify class and gender inequalities that have a sociopolitical basis. Research concerned with egalitarian ideals for education needs to problematize 'ability' by examining the social context that defines pupils' situations within the school institution. That is a sociological task *par excellence*. It is, appropriate, therefore, that in the next chapter I consider some of the main sociological contributions in this field before discussing my own empirical study.

Chapter 2

Sociology of Education and Secondary Schooling

What follows is a critical survey of the main theoretical and empirical contributions to the sociology of secondary education. This helps to clarify and contextualize the complexity of the investigations undertaken later.

Academic Achievement, Schooling and Social Class

It was not until the 1960s that sociology gained widespread establishment as a discipline in British universities, but the research of Hogben (1938) and his colleagues marked the beginning of a tradition of sociology of education in Britain. As described in their major publication, *Political Arithmetic: a symposium of population studies*, they were concerned with the underutilization of people's 'ability' as a result of social and institutional inefficiency:

> . . . the problem of political arithmetic is to estimate the remedial wastage due to defective social organization and the loss of social efficiency resulting from them. (Hogben, 1938, p. 332)

Hogben was committed to this research because he wished to eliminate such 'social wastage', and because he believed it would offer scope for further enquiry concerning social class, mobility and social structure. Typically this research would control for the variable 'ability' as translated by 'intelligence' tests in order to set up interclass comparisons. Some of their results showed that many schoolchildren lacked access to higher education because of their parents' incomes rather than because of their lack of 'ability'. Such results implied major policy changes if 'equality of educational opportunity' was to be implemented.

Policy changes did come. In 1941 the Norwood Committee declared that they had discovered three types of child and this was the forebearer for the three-tier secondary-school system defined by the 1944 Education Act in England and Wales. At the age of 11 pupils were to be selected for grammar schools (academic), secondary modern (vocational) and technical college (shorter skill-oriented training) (Lawson and Silver, 1973). The three types of school were not viewed with equal prestige. The successes in the 11 + test went to the grammar school and the failures were destined for the secondary-modern schools.

Sociologists were at the forefront of exposing that the proclaimed 'equality of opportunity' which the 1944 Act was supposed to provide had not materialized. Glass (1954) and Floud, Halsey and Martin (1966) came to focus on what factors gave rise to the relative underachievement of working-class children in schools despite the provisions of the Education Act. They pointed to massive under-representation of working-class boys at grammar schools. Further research showed that working-class pupils gained fewer grammar-school places than middle-class children with the same IQ and that teachers' assessments in primary schools were biased in favour of middle-class pupils independently of social-class biases in the IQ tests themselves (Douglas, 1964).

Important as these early studies were, they left a great deal unquestioned. They only compared 'inputs' such as social class, 'aptitudes', 'giftedness' and 'intelligence' with 'outputs' such as further education, examination achievement and occupations. This resulted in a focus of attention on parental attitudes and home background at the expense of any real understanding of how schools might affect children's performance. In particular, they threw no light on the cultural aspects of schooling. If working-class culture did have differences from middle-class culture in the home and in the community then we would expect some of these to be significant in the everyday activities of schools. More significantly, in considering the provisions of the 1944 Education Act it was important to establish whether the secondary-level schools as institutions accentuated or reduced pre-existing social-class differences in achievement.

It was not until Jackson and Marsden (1962) that an in-depth study of the generation and consequences of the differences between working-class and middle-class cultures in relation to education became available. They used small samples (ten middle-class families and eighty-eight working-class families) by comparison with the earlier demographic work in an attempt to 'go behind the numbers and feel a way into the various human situations they represent' (Jackson and Marsden, 1962, p. 13). The ninety-eight men and women studied had all successfully travelled the path of grammar school, college, university and middle-class professions. The bias in the sample towards working-class men and women indicates the researchers' particular interest in how travelling this educational path was felt by the working-class child. Like Douglas, Floud and Glass, they sought explanations of why the upper reaches of the grammar school were dominated by middle-class children in a predominantly working-class town.

The message of the book was that there was a clash between the two class cultures specifically in the arena of the school and the neighbourhood. The grammar schools were founded, and often staffed, by the local middle-class. This meant that there was a trusting understanding between the school and family supporting the middle-class child. By contrast, for the working-class children entrance into the grammar school was characterized by insecurity, confusion and a lack of belonging. For these children grammar-school life departed sharply from their way of life in their neighbourhood. They experienced a heightened sense of separateness since the majority of working-class children who would fail the 11 + test would be sent to entirely different schools. Thus, in the face of intense competition for educational success at the grammar school, these working-class children experienced a clash of loyalties between school and neighbourhood. For the first time sociology of education indicated that the school contributed to the dilemmas, anxieties and educational performance of working-class children compared with their middle-class peers. Nevertheless, much more research of this kind remained to be developed since Jackson and Marsden had only concentrated on highly successful grammar-school pupils.[1]

The organizational and ethnographic studies of schools in the North of England by Hargreaves (1967) and Lacey (1970) followed. Together these spanned the whole 'failure' to 'success' spectrum from boys in the bottom 'ability' streams of the low-status secondary moderns to boys in the top streams of the high-status grammar schools. Lacey, for example, undertook an extensive study of one boys' grammar school. Like Jackson and Marsden, his aim was to explain and clarify the social mechanisms that account for the correlation between social class and educational achievement. Essentially Lacey established a model describing various social processes characteristic of the boys' passage through the school. That model depended on a positive relationship between a boy's academic performance and his behaviour, and on the development of two concepts 'differentiation' and 'polarization'. He defined differentiation as 'the separation and ranking of students according to a multiple set of criteria which make up the normative academically oriented value systems of the grammar school'; and polarization as a process which 'takes place within the student body, partly as a result of differentiation, but influenced by external factors and with an autonomy of its own. It is a process of subculture formation in which the school-dominated normative culture is opposed to an alternative culture which I refer to as the "anti-group culture"' (Lacey, 1970, p. 57).

Differentiation was carried out by teachers and the school establishment whereas polarization took place among the pupils because of differentiation. Hargreaves and Lacey contend that the system of streaming pupils was a major cause of the development of anti-academic attitudes amongst those pupils labelled as failures by the school establishment. By contrast, they found that pupils labelled as successes by the academic value system of the school tended to exhibit pro-school and pro-academic attitudes. Consequently, from these studies emerged the theory that academic differentiation by the school creates a polarization of subcultures within the pupil population, those dominated by pro-school values and those dominated by anti-school value — 'the differentiation–polarization theory' (Hammersley, 1985).

Importantly, Lacey further claims that the twin processes of differentiation and polarization were associated with social-class differentiation. Middle-class boys were found to be disproportionately successful according to the academic values of the school *and* predominantly affiliated themselves to pro-school subcultures. Working-class boys, on the other hand, were found to fail disproportionately and were more likely to develop anti-school attitudes. Anti-school values, argues Lacey, tended to lead to a pupil's decrease in academic achievement. Hence, he concludes that through academic differentiation the school did indeed contribute to the social-class differences in academic achievement.

Woods (1979) extended the organizational case-study approach to a study of a mixed secondary-modern school in the Midlands. He identified various 'group perspectives' amongst parents, pupils and staff, and found that there were social-class differences in how pupils and parents approached important decisions about opting for school subjects. These class differences were mediated by the streaming within the school. The predominantly middle-class form 3A pupils were particularly well informed about the importance of subject-option choice for their futures as compared with the mainly working-class 3C. Social-class differences were also found in other aspects of the pupils' school lives, such as their views of the curriculum, institutional rules and teaching techniques.

Large-scale comprehensivization meant that the predominantly working-class intakes of secondary-modern schools were combined with the intakes of grammar schools. Even though streaming continued in many comprehensives (Pedley, 1969), it was usually less rigid than in the grammar and secondary-modern schools. It is important to note, therefore, that Ball (1981) found that the differentiation–polarization theory also held true in a mixed comprehensive school with looser streaming by banding.

Limitations of Organizational Studies

A major criticism of the early ethnographic studies of Hargreaves and Lacey was that they had neglected to ask questions about the content of education. Their accounts did not consider the issue of what the content of education should be about — the nature of school knowledge. Although Ball and Woods both studied the organization of school knowledge they focused on how the school processed pupils with respect to knowledge categories rather than how it processed the knowledge itself.

The early studies can also be criticized for neglecting the study of girls' subcultures or at least failing to acknowledge that similar processes might not occur with girls. However, Ball and Woods appear to have compensated for this to some extent by studying mixed schools. In particular, Ball seems to have substantiated the differentiation–polarization theory for boys and girls. On the other hand, Lambart (1976), studying a sample of girls in a grammar school, found that some of the high-achieving girls were also the worst behaved. This finding is directly opposed to the differentiation–polarization theory. Also Furlong (1976), who studied a group of schoolgirls, argues that pupils are not significantly influenced by persistent subcultural norms and values in the ways suggested by Hargreaves and Lacey. He claims that pupil behaviour is much more situationally determined and suggests that 'interaction set' more accurately describes friendship groupings of pupils than 'subculture'. In relation to this Davies (1984) has suggested that Furlong's findings were different to Hargreaves's and Lacey's because he was studying girls.

It is important, then, that further organizational studies are designed so as to take account of sex differences. Yet studying mixed schools and samples of girls as well as boys in order to explore social-class differences is not the same as exploring sex differences and gender differences. On the whole, Ball and Woods did not investigate gender as an organizing category in their research. Feminists, in particular, have criticized many organizational studies for neglecting gender as a dynamic in the process of secondary schooling.

A further problem is that, because these organizational studies are all case-studies, generalizations need to be made with care. For example, how far can we generalize Lacey's differentiation–polarization theory to comprehensives? These problems have been partly tackled because of Ball's confirmation of the theory in a comprehensive school. He studied a comprehensive in the South of England that was streamed by 'banding', which involves a broad streaming of cross-subject forms. However, in a survey of two comprehensives, Quine (1974) found that there was little evidence to support the differentiation–polarization theory. On the basis of the memoranda and pupil-interview data collected by two research assistants during the course of one year of participant observation, Quine reports that the pupils labelled as trouble makers tended to be in the top stream and that the pupils in the bottom streams accepted and liked the school regime.

The comprehensives studied by Quine differed from Ball's Beachside Comprehensive in two important ways. The first is that their intakes, like those of Hargreaves's secondary modern were almost entirely (95 per cent) working-class. It might be postulated that Quine's different results were due to this factor because an absence of social-class culture conflict among the pupil population inhibited polarization. However, this seems implausible since Hargreaves's secondary modern had a similar intake. The second is that Quine's comprehensives were streamed by 'setting' rather than banding.[2] Setting entails streaming into subject-based classes. Whether this organizational difference can account for the differences in findings remains an open question, but as I shall discuss further in Chapter 4 there are good reasons for supposing that the differentiation–polarization theory can also apply to setted comprehensives.

School Knowledge and Social Class

The emphasis on school knowledge within educational studies owes much to the attempt by Young (1971) to incorporate theoretical ideas from the sociology of knowledge into the sociology of education. By all accounts his edited collection *Knowledge and Control: New Directions for the Sociology of Education* earmarked the beginning of the 'new' sociology of education. He argued that knowledge as well as people were processed in schools, and that studies of schooling should begin with an appreciation of the interrelationship between the two. Young claimed that this could be achieved by considering how knowledge areas, and in particular school subjects, are socially constructed. Following the phenomenological prescriptions of Schutz (1967), he advocated that knowledge should be treated as an intersubjective reality which people have constructed to give meaning to their world.

The various strands within the sociology of school knowledge can be thought of as falling into three categories: theories of the social construction of school knowledge; theories of the organization of knowledge transmission; and studies of the social-class stratification of school knowledge. These categories are not, of course, mutually exclusive and arguably all the contributors to this new paradigm were concerned about the social-class stratification of school knowledge.

The first category includes Young's three dimensional model of the knowledge content of curricula and his general phenomenological theory focusing on how different social groups define legitimate knowledge and, therefore, how school knowledge is determined. The first dimension is 'scope' (specialization), which defines the restriction of accessibility of knowledge areas to different groups of people. The second, openness, refers to the relatedness of certain knowledge areas. And the third, stratification, is a function of the power of some groups to define the social value of certain areas of knowledge. Young claims that all these dimensions can, and should, be explained by the sociology of education as part of a critical exploration into what counts as knowledge.

Bernstein (1971) is the main contributor to the second category. He provides us with a plethora of concepts with which to study the social organization of formal educational knowledge. The two most important ones are classification, which refers to the degree of distinctiveness between contents, and framing, which refers to the degree of control teachers and pupils possess over the selection and pacing of the knowledge transmitted and received in a pedogogical relationship. Classification is an especially useful idea to bear in mind when comparing educational practices in different subjects (or knowledge systems) whilst framing has obvious connections with organizational differentiation such as streaming versus mixed-ability classes.

Under the third category fall two empirical studies carried out by Keddie (1971) and Anyon (1981). By comparing the actions of teachers as theorizers in the 'educationist context' and as practitioners in the classroom (the 'teacher context') Keddie showed how an 'undifferentiated' humanities curriculum package supported, in principle, by the teachers became differentiated, in practice, across different streams. Certain curriculum contents were deemed beyond the 'bottom' stream (mostly working-class). Their inability to cope with material considered appropriate for the 'top' stream (mainly middle-class) was often explained in terms of home background. The implication of Keddie's study is that school knowledge is differentiated on the basis of social class mediated by organizational factors such as streaming. Anyon's study was slightly different in that it postulated knowledge differentiation between working-class schools and middle-class schools. Anyon found that the school teachers had quite different expectations of what the pupils should know about in the different schools and used curriculum materials accordingly. Amongst the many sociological implications of this work is the contribution that a division of educational knowledge based on social class makes to the division of labour in the wider class society.

Drawbacks of the 'New' Sociology of Educational Knowledge

There appear to be several internal inconsistencies in the approach of this programme. Despite Young's allusions to interrelating studies of how school knowledge is constructed with other organizational research, the programme became defined as a 'new' paradigm to be distinguished from 'traditional' studies of schooling. For example, Gorbutt (1972) celebrated the 'new' programme's shedding of the following three characteristics of the 'traditional' paradigm:

the belief that educational research can be a value-free science;

that educational research has the capacity to 'discover fundamental truths through objective techniques of empirical investigation'; and

that the extent of objectivity of data is directly proportional to the statistical sophistication of the research.

These views were supported by Young (1973) who claimed that an inevitable consequence of 'treating what counts as knowledge as problematic' is the renunciation of explicit truth criteria, that is, epistemological relativism.

The problems of vagueness and epistemological relativism implied by this 'new' programme have been exposed by Pring (1972). What precisely could be subsumed under the sociological explanations of school knowledge? Would this include logical relations within disciplines? If so, then is it assumed that all structures of knowledge are reducible to sociological explanations? Furthermore, if epistemological relativism is to guide the programme then how will it ever know that its own explanations are plausible? Pring contends that the sociology of educational knowledge cannot explain what counts as knowledge because if it is based on epistemological relativism it will have no way of distinguishing that which is known from that which is not (including whether or not its own explanations contribute to knowledge). Gorbutt is correct to suggest that sociology of education is not value-free, but it does not follow from this that it cannot reveal truths via empirical investigation. It may be that some truths, especially those that threaten the *status quo* are more effectively discovered from a value-committed position (Abraham, 1994). Moreover, it is not accurate to represent the more 'traditional' research in sociology of education as applying solely quantitative methods.

Whitty (1985, p. 22), a critical supporter of the sociology of educational knowledge, has acknowledged that the initial orientation of the 'new' paradigm 'was both theoretically and practically flawed'. However, he makes this remark almost in passing as one possible reason why neo-Marxist approaches to school knowledge became more influential within the paradigm. Indeed, for Whitty, the main weakness of the paradigm in the early and mid-1970s was that it tended to neglect the relationship between curriculum change and capitalist society. He may be right to point out this deficiency, but he does not tackle adequately the epistemological problems identified by Pring, describing them as 'not of overwhelming significance' (Whitty, 1985, p. 15). Others go further and suppose that the philosophical weaknesses of the 'new' paradigm are irrelevant because what really matters is whether the 'new' theories advance the cause of radical educational practices.

They are wrong to be so dismissive. These philosophical inconsistencies are significant and resolving them has important implications for our understanding of the stratification of school knowledge and hence possible curriculum changes. A coherent philosophy is required, though not sufficient, to identify areas of agreement and dispute, and to make decisions about the direction of educational change. This is especially true when consensus about practice is lacking. A major difficulty with applying the suggestions of the 'new' paradigm in practice is the apparently all encompassing role of knowledge. For example, Young (1973, p. 214) maintains that the 'new' paradigm 'starts by rejecting the assumption of any superiority of educational or "academic" knowledge over the everyday commonsense knowledge available to people as being in the world'. However, the assumption that some knowledge is superior to other knowledge requires people in some social system to make such an assumption. Young's comment, therefore, has little to do with the nature of the knowledge and more to do with the social process of attributing status to various skills/knowledge. Similarly, as Demaine (1981) notes, the pertinent finding of Keddie's study was not the superiority or inferiority of certain knowledge systems, but rather the status given to the knowledge. When Young argues that making what counts as school knowledge problematic implies epistemological relativism he appears to be conflating knowledge (things we know about) with the social status of knowledge (how social groups, institutions, or societies reward and value certain knowledge). If these two categories are kept distinct, then Young's desire to explore the social stratification of knowledge need not require the abandonment of truth criteria at all.

Philosophical inconsistencies also give rise to ambiguities in empirical studies of the stratification of school knowledge. This, in turn, creates difficulties in making progress with the project of a 'working class curriculum' (Whitty, 1985, p. 68). For example, consider the research by Anyon (1981) purporting to demonstrate social-class bias in the school curriculum in the USA. She compares four types of schools: 'working-class schools', 'middle-class schools', 'affluent professional schools' and 'executive elite schools' and claims to have revealed two aspects of school knowledge which she calls 'reproductive' and 'non-reproductive':

> 'Reproductive' will refer to aspects of school knowledge that contribute directly to the legitimation and perpetuation of ideologies, practices, and privileges constitutive of present economic and political structures. 'Non-reproductive' knowledge is that which facilitates fundamental transformation of ideologies, practices on the basis of which objects, services, and ideas (and other cultural products) are produced, owned, distributed, and publicly evaluated. (Anyon, 1981, pp. 31–2)

According to Anyon, in the 'working-class schools' school knowledge is 'reproductive' because the working-class students are neither taught about working-class history nor offered the knowledge and skills which would enable them to further their own class interests. Her observations about the absence of accounts of working-class history in curricular texts may well be accurate. What is less clear is whether she believes that such absence results in an intrinsically inferior form of knowledge. Her discussion of elite schools is suggestive of an intrinsic hierarchy of knowledge:

> The data suggest that knowledge in this executive elite school is academic, intellectual and rigorous. There is an attempt to teach

more and more *difficult* concepts than in any other school. (Anyon,
1981, p. 31, my emphasis)

In what sense are these concepts 'difficult' and for whom? This is an
important question because, according to Anyon, it is 'conceptual knowledge' that students in the 'working-class schools' are wholly or partially
denied.

Yet it remains unclear whether Anyon is claiming that the knowledge
content of the curriculum has some intrinsic 'reproductive' effects. Much
more clarity about the nature of school knowledge than Anyon provides
is needed if alternative formulations, such as a curriculum containing
'really useful knowledge' are to be well informed (Johnson, 1979; Whitty,
1985).

Academic Achievement, Gender and School Knowledge

One major criticism of the two paradigm approaches in the sociology of
education considered so far is that they have concentrated on the social-
class characteristics of education at the expense of gender. As Blackstone
(1976) notes, academic sociology neglected gender as a source of social
differentiation. According to Acker (1981) this neglect is particularly marked
in British sociology of education. For example, in a study of journal articles in the field of empirical sociology of education she found that a large
minority (37 per cent) had all-male samples while only 5 per cent had all-
female samples. Nevertheless, evidence has been accumulating within feminist literature of substantial gender differentiation of school knowledge.
For example, a survey of mixed comprehensive schooling in 1970 found
that in half of the schools considered some subjects were reserved only for
boys and 49 per cent *also* limited some subjects to girls only (Deem, 1978,
p. 19).

As a result of the Sex Discrimination Act of 1975 compulsory differential curricula for boys and girls were virtually outlawed. Nevertheless,
the curious phenomenon of girls opting out of mathematical, scientific
and technological subjects and boys opting out of arts, humanities and
languages remained. Furthermore, feminists have argued that girls suffer
academically generally at school due to the prevalence of sexism in language and reward systems (Spender and Sarah, 1988; Delamont, 1990).

Blackstone (1976) and Kelly (1981) offer some insights into the extent
of these phenomena. They found that at the age of 16 girls performed no
worse than their male peers in public examinations in Britain. It was not
until the 'A' level stage that major differences in performance between
the sexes arose, but this was because girls entered for fewer 'A' levels
not because they had a lower pass rate. And secondly, in England and
Wales relative to their participation in school subjects as a whole, girls

were significantly under-represented in the physical sciences from the fourth year of secondary school onwards. However, given this under-representation in the physical sciences, girls did not give up their study of science at later stages with a rate any greater than they did for other subjects. Thus the crucial period in which the under-representation of girls' participation in physical science occurred was in the fourth year. This was confirmed in a major survey by Pratt, Bloomfield and Seale (1984) as follows:

> At the fourth-form option stage, boys were found mostly in physics and chemistry and girls in biology; more boys than girls were taking two science subjects; in languages (French and German) girls predominated. A slightly higher proportion of boys than girls took geography and more girls than boys took history; proportionately more girls than boys were studying music . . . the predominance of boys in physics and chemistry raised important questions about the content of scientific studies followed. Again, the preponderance of girls taking French and German suggests boys may equally miss opportunities in the field of modern languages. (Pratt, Bloomfield and Seale, 1984: 6)

Sociological explanations for these sex differences range from analyses of curriculum materials and pupil–teacher interaction to studies of peer-group pressure and pupil anxiety. Whyld (1983) demonstrates that textbooks show men in a great variety of work roles while adult women tend to be cast in the role of wife or mother. She claims that subjects and textbooks are sex-stereotyped. Some studies suggest that secondary teachers prefer to teach boys rather than girls because boys are perceived to be more interesting, and that this may have deleterious effects on the achievement of girls (Weiner, 1980).

There are many other studies on similar themes. All of them tend to argue that pupils' success in various areas of school knowledge depends on either 'role models' provided by 'significant others' (e.g., teachers, characters in textbooks) or frameworks of sex-stereotyping due to teacher and pupil labelling (e.g., 'science is a boys' subject'). One criticism of these studies is that the relationship between pupils' achievement in subjects and 'role modelling' is usually assumed rather than demonstrated. Relationships between school knowledge and gender development are extremely complex and we do not yet have a clear picture of the mechanisms involved. Although the nature of the problem may be such that research findings are inevitably 'messy', it is important not to replace explanations with assertions.

There is also a massive bias in the literature on subject sex-stereotyping concerned with the relative under-participation of girls in mathematical, scientific and technological subjects, but little concern about explaining boys' lack of uptake in arts and languages. As Davies (1984) notes, funding for research projects such as 'Girls Into Science and Technology' (GIST) exist in order to convince girls, teachers and employers that girls are as able as boys to tackle technical subjects. This research has tended to neglect wider political issues which bear on the desirability of current scientific enterprises.

For example, Saraga and Griffiths (1981) argue that the science learnt in schools reflects the motivations and requirements of a male-dominated military-industrial complex with capitalist interests. They suggest that the problem of male dominance in science should not be formulated in terms of how to encourage girls to participate more fully and successfully in school science but rather of how to transform the exploitative social relations which have characterized the development of science. On a similar theme Easlea (1981) and Bently and Watts (1987) maintain that science and the scientific mode of enquiry inspired by the Scientific Revolution of the seventeenth century are intrinsically masculine.

Although it can be objected that science is much more variable than these critics imply (Kelly, 1988), it does seem clear that research into the participation of girls in science should explicitly recognize other social, economic and political forces at work as well as those pressing to eliminate sex discrimination. That is, the tendency towards a more technocratic society in which questions of cultural identity and human values are subordinated to technical efficacy. There are, as yet, no 'Boys Into Child Care' research projects nor 'Boys and Learning Languages Associations' and this may reflect their inability to contribute to a more technocratic society as well as resistance to changing gender relations.

Gender Relations and Schooling

It is not possible to separate the relationships between boys and girls at school from their respective academic achievement in school subjects in any rigid way. Nor is it the case that gender relations between pupils in the classroom are unrelated to knowledge differentiation (Frasier and Sadker, 1973; Kelly, 1985). In fact, theories of gender reproduction emphasize the interactive relationship between external reality and individual-internalization processes of feminity and masculinity. School subjects become gendered through a 'gender code', which serves to recontextualize appropriate gendered behaviour in the family to appropriate gendered academic disciplines in schools (MacDonald, 1980).

Having said this, for analytical purposes, it is possible to separate analyses of the gendered aspects of schooling which concentrate on academic achievement and school knowledge from those which focus on the informal and cultural aspects of school life. Included in this latter group are studies of sexuality, gender identity, the gendered aspects of adolescent discourse, and 'subcultural' norms of masculine and feminine behaviour that do not relate so directly to school subjects.

Studies of adolescent sexuality have been rare in the sociology of education even among feminist research. Willis (1977), however, was one of the first in-depth ethnographic studies to include a discussion of masculinity and sexism within a boys' 'counter-school' subculture. To some extent Willis illuminates certain gender relations in the school. In particular, he reports how the working-class 'counter-school' boys (known to themselves and others as 'the lads') were, on the whole sexist, manualist and machismo. They also claimed to be (hetero)sexually experienced. By contrast, the 'conformists' are reported as fairly inept in their relationships with girls.

Those findings are supported by Wood (1984) who gives an account of some working-class boys' sexism towards girls in a centre for school 'disruptives' by considering their sexual practices and sexual fantasies as well as the meanings they attach to derogatory terms used to label girls. He found that terms such as 'dogs', 'horny birds' and 'right whores' all carried meanings comprising complex assessments and value judgments about girls' bodies and behaviour. Wood also documents how these assumptions about what girls 'really want' in their relationships with boys are transformed into intrusive sexual practices during unsupervised periods of 'playful' groping. Mahoney (1985) also encountered cases of girls being physically molested by boys inside and outside the classroom.

Girls do not just complain about unwanted physical invasion. As Lee (1983) notes, sexual language can be particularly hurtful to adolescents who are unsure about their gender identity and sexual expectations. The impact of sexist language on girls' subcultures has been explored by Lees (1993). She argues that boys' terms of sexual abuse, especially 'slag', have controlling effects on girls' behaviour. While the girls do not welcome this sexual abuse they contribute to their own situation by accepting certain norms of patriarchal society, and by bowing to the force of certain structural constraints put on them by patriarchal relations.

This research has two important implications for schooling apart from in the obvious area of 'sex education' in schools. First, as Mahoney (1985, pp. 46–7) graphically describes sexist language and assumptions can affect the verbal participation of girls and boys in the classroom and their relationships with teachers. And secondly, schools represent specific sites of sexism with their particular kinds of organization. This means that sexism in schools should not be reduced to a sexism which is merely a by-product of a particular culture as Willis (1977) seems to suggest. Mahoney notes that in many cases sexist activities seemed to arise out of sheer boredom within school. Sexism in schools derives from a combination of extra-school cultural tendencies and specifically intra-school structures and situations. This points to the need to combine some of the insights of feminist research on patriarchal culture with organizational studies of schools.

Theories of Reproduction: Correspondence and Resistance

These theories are firmly rooted in the neo-Marxist tradition within the sociology of education. The best known advocates of 'correspondence' theories of schooling are Bowles and Gintis (1976), who claim that ethnographic studies of schooling fail to confront the basic problem of schooling, namely its role in reproducing capitalist relations. This is because they believe that the school acts merely to reproduce and legitimate social relations of dominance, subordination and motivation in the economic sphere.

On this view schools induce people to accept the degree of powerlessness with which they will be faced as mature workers. A major weakness of this approach is that it considers all the political aspects of schooling to be generated by their location in capitalist society. This is scarcely true since schools have considerable institutional autonomy in liberal democracies. Arguably ethnographic studies of schools help us to identify which social and political processes are bounded by this autonomy, which are rigidly attached to the wider social and political structure, and which are somewhere in between.

Although Bowles and Gintis devote a great deal of analysis to how the social relations of schooling contain structural correspondents to the social relations of production, they tend to neglect the reproduction of school knowledge. This is the emphasis of Bourdieu (1973) who explains how schooling can reproduce inequalities in 'cultural capital' by stratifying school knowledge. According to Bourdieu, school knowledge is differentiated into that which is appropriate for 'high-status' culture and that which is appropriate for 'low-status' culture. Reproduction of cultural inequality occurs partly because within the education system middle-class pupils are given much more access to 'high-status' knowledge than working-class pupils. It is, of course, important to note that 'high status' and 'low status' are defined within the current power relations of society, and that the activities of middle classes come to be defined as 'high status' partly because of their power status.

A persistent criticism of correspondence theories is that they underplay human agency in the social processes of schooling. In particular, Gaskell (1985) argues that it cannot be assumed that pupils internalize the dominant ideological messages of the school. She proposes that working-class girls may wish to 'drop out' of academic studies for good reasons that are not part of ideological transmission. The research by Willis (1981) also emphasizes the importance of capturing pupils' agency. He claims that the process of socio-cultural reproduction is not a smooth one. Pupils do not passively accept the social positions allocated to them in the school system but they *resist* the system. Willis maintains that such resistance is of particular social-class significance and that the active resistance of working-class 'kids' to schooling is a major causative factor in reproducing their social-class position in the wider socio-economic sphere. In essence, Willis suggests that working-class 'kids' contribute, reproductively, to their own destiny by their cultural resistance to the school.

The theme of working-class resistance to schooling has been taken up by other neo-Marxists such as Corrigan (1979) and Humphries (1981). Common to their expositions is the idea that the introduction of compulsory state schooling was a cultural imposition on the working class designed to produce an orderly and disciplined workforce, and to legitimate class inequalities. Corrigan suggests that education is still conceived in terms of 'changing working-class culture' and that the consequence is working-class resistance.' Thus, anti-school behaviour is interpreted as cultural resistance — a form of class-conscious rebellion against the education system.

For Willis that culture of resistance has creative tendencies and a certain degree of autonomous freedom, which has the potential to challenge the reproduction of social-class relations in capitalist society. In this sense, working-class cultural resistance to schooling is a contradictory phenomenon: it challenges and creates socio-cultural reproduction. The challenge lies in the domain of 'cultural production' which, Willis argues, was overlooked by the theorists who presented reproduction as a fairly smooth process.

Resistance Theory Re-evaluated

Willis's work has been influential and celebrated by much of the resistance-theory literature. Giroux (1983a, 1983b) is one of the most prolific resistance theorists so in this section I discuss mainly his work. In seeking to elaborate the concept of resistance Giroux discusses its meaning, the relationship between resistance and political change and future research investigations. Unfortunately theoretical development is hampered by a persistent reluctance to treat these matters with sufficient distinctiveness.

For example, he rejects theories of cultural reproduction because '[b]y downplaying the importance of human agency and the notion of resistance, reproduction theories offer little hope for challenging and changing the repressive features of schooling' (Giroux, 1983a, p. 259). Evidently Giroux is willing to reject theories because they are not politically optimistic irrespective of whether the theory informs us about the social world. When it comes to his prescriptions for future research related difficulties arise. Giroux proposes that 'oppositional behaviour needs to be analysed to 'see if it constitutes a form of resistance, which . . . means uncovering its emancipatory interests'. (Giroux, 1983b, p. 110) Yet he also claims:

> One of the most important assumptions of resistance theory is that working class students are not merely the by-product of capital, compliantly submitting to the dictates of authoritarian teachers

and schools that prepare them for a life of deadening labour. Rather, schools represent contested terrains marked not only by structural and ideological contradictions but also by collectively informed student resistance. (Giroux, 1983a, p. 260)

This latter quote implies that resistance theory does not examine 'oppositional behaviour' to explore whether it constitutes resistance, but rather it operates on the prior assumption that schools' authority is challenged by 'collectively informed student resistance'. However, it is not obvious that this is a defensible assumption if only because of the lack of clarity in defining resistance within resistance theories (Giroux, 1983b, p. 108, p. 289). Giroux's working definition of resistance is as follows:

> . . . the nature and meaning of an act of resistance *has* to be defined next to the degree to which it contains the possibilities to develop what Marcuse termed 'a commitment to an emancipation of sensibility, imagination, and reason in all spheres of subjectivity and objectivity'. (Giroux, 1983b, p. 108)

It is not clear from this extremely broad definition what might count as a possibility to develop a commitment to emancipation. An optimist might argue that almost any human situation contains such a 'possibility' no matter how remote.

The great drawback of such a broad definition in empirical studies is that almost anything counts as resistance. For instance, Anyon (1981, p. 11) refers to 'active and passive resistance'. According to her, active resistance involves attempts to sabotage the teacher's control in the class (e.g., by putting a bug in another student's desk) whilst passive resistance can be merely not responding to a teacher's question, or not showing enthusiasm for the classroom proceedings. If resistance is identified simply by observing lack of response to teachers' questions then it is so broad in scope that its significance as a *distinct* cultural form is surely rather small. Yet from this kind of data she concludes that the working-class resistors had 'seen through the system' (Anyon, 1981, p. 32). Such 'Left idealism' tends to see the deviant behaviour of working-class pupils as proto-revolutionary action and looks to such behaviour for hints of radical political change (Furlong, 1985, pp. 168–72).

A study by Aggleton and Whitty (1985) has helped resistance theory move beyond the definitional deficiencies identified above. They make the useful distinction between 'resistance' (challenges against pervasive power relations in wider society) and 'contestations' (challenges against localized principles of control). These definitions are much clearer than those of other resistance theorists. However, resistance theory may have a price to pay in terms of its significance for this clarity. Using these more precise definitions, Aggleton and Whitty concluded that 'contestation', but not 'resistance' characterized the middle-class students whom they studied.

The way in which resistance theory was derived from the ethnography of Willis (1977) has also drawn considerable criticism not least because he allowed his study of boys to generate a theory about working-class 'kids' (girls and boys) thus ignoring any possible sex differences that might limit the theory. Leaving this aside Walker (1985, 1986) argues that Willis's conclusion that 'the lads' were resistors is not supported by his own ethnographic data except by reading into it a theory which claims a dualism of observable appearances and unobservable essences. This dualism, argues Walker, is crucial to Willis's resistance theory because the socially progressive/revolutionary aspects of 'the lads' counter-school culture (what Willis calls 'penetrations') do not manifest themselves in the data (i.e., at the level of appearances). Indeed Walker suggests that if Willis's data imply anything about working-class culture then they illustrate its reproductive elements. Walker maintains that Willis's dualism enables him to propose that the 'penetrations' exist in *essence* despite the data. According to Willis, 'the lads' are better described as recusants rather than resistors. Recusancy is merely opposing elements of a system but *not* necessarily wanting to see the system replaced by another one — usually thought of as a defining feature of resistance.

Thus, basing resistance theory on Willis's study may be a hazardous undertaking. On the other hand, Willis does emphasize the ultimate reproductive consequences of 'the lads' culture. Walker does not seem to give this point sufficient airing.

A Synthesis and a Framework

If sociology of education is to be informative and useful it must be committed to truth and accuracy. There do need to be criteria by which to judge the validity of knowledge claims. Otherwise sociology of education cannot provide valid or reliable knowledge about gender and/or class inequality or indeed about any other aspect of schooling. That is to say, objectivity is a necessary condition for an intelligible sociological enterprise. However, this does not imply that sociological investigation must be value-free.

This requirement should not be confused with the proposal that sociology of education should be indifferent to making a contribution to political change. The importance of having valid research with which to inform programmes for social transformation is noted succinctly by Lukes:

> It is only by assuming that one has a reliable, non-relative means of identifying a disjunction between social consciousness or collective representations on the one hand and social realities on the

other that one can raise questions about the ways in which belief-systems prevent or promote social change. (Lukes, 1973, p. 243)

Those who wish to see a radical change in the social order need reliable knowledge. As Johnson recounts, radicals of the early nineteenth century were well aware of the desirability of searching for the truth about the social world as a guide for their radical politics:

> Despite the stress on a relation to the knower's experience, there is no narrowly *pragmatic* conception of knowledge here. Knowledge is not just a political instrument; the search for 'truth' matters . . . Certain truths had a pressing immediacy. They were indispensable means to emancipation. (Johnson, 1979, p. 86)

Thus, values may guide, but not determine, research outcomes. The notion of value-free social science is worthless because no research is value-free *per se*. Rather research can be demonstrated to be free from *specific* values that are claimed to underlie it (Keat, 1981). This is very important because it prevents values and knowledge from collapsing into one another (as occurred with the epistemological relativism espoused by the 'new' sociologists of education), while acknowledging that values do in general play a role in social-science research. In this sense it is possible and necessary to develop a value-committed objective sociology of education.

This position is consistent with the realism proposed by Sharp and Green (1975). Such realism implies that the conceptual distinction between reality and actors' accounts of reality should be retained. It also leads to an empirical-research emphasis somewhat different from the 'perspectivism' that dominates many symbolic interactionist and social constructionist studies of education. The latter merely present an array of perspectives or 'social constructions', but are reluctant to make judgments about the validity of those perspectives because they reject the idea of an objective reality.

My approach is to explore the various perspectives of pupils and teachers in school, but also to appreciate the incompleteness and limitations of those perspectives. As the organizational studies of Lacey and Hargreaves have shown, other sources of data such as official school records, curricular materials and the researcher's field observations help to inform us about the reality of the situation in which the actors are operating. In short, it is important to take account of structure and agency, and to acknowledge that agents may be ignorant or oblivious of structures that affect their lives (Abraham, 1994).

This point has significant implications for resistance studies in sociology of education because it warns against *presupposing* that working-class anti-school pupils are conscious of the structural consequences of schooling for their social-class members. When anti-school behaviour and polarization from pro-school values are found, there remains the empirical question of whether class-based resistance is also present. It is yet a further step to suppose that resistance is a form of opposition to capitalism. Even if it is accepted that the formal education system was established to change working-class culture into a workforce for capitalism, pupils' opposition to that education system might merely reflect resistance to change rather than specifically to capitalism. Substantial direct empirical evidence, to date not forthcoming, is required to support the 'Left idealist' thesis. Similar arguments apply to how the deviant behaviour of sociologists should be interpreted, and to the prospects of them resisting patriarchy.

Nevertheless, elaborating the mechanisms of gender and class divisions remains important. From previous work in sociology we have learnt that organizational streaming and the stratification of knowledge are key aspects of secondary schooling that may sensitize us to the dynamics of class division in education. Furthermore, feminist researchers have revealed that gender differentiation needs to be examined at the levels of social relationships in school life, the organization of school knowledge and curricular texts. These should be key investigative targets when focusing on gender divisions in school. However, it is important not to naturalize gender divisions by reducing them to sex differences. Gender differences between members of the *same* sex are worthy of exploration.

Notes

1   Though the social-class culture clash thesis appears to be widely substantiated in the sociology of education it has not gone entirely unchallenged. For example, Witkin (1974) rejects the thesis of Jackson and Marsden (1962) on the basis of his findings.
2   Burgess (1983) also studied a setted comprehensive school but he was concerned with the organizational provisions made by the school for early school leavers with special reference to the Newsom Report.

Chapter 3

Research Methodology and Design

In tackling the question of gender and class divisions in comprehensive schooling I undertook a case-study of an individual school because I wanted to explore the relevant social processes in depth. To help me focus this interest I employed the concepts of differentiation and polarization. These were first developed by Lacey (1970), but I have modified his definitions (Chapter 2) to allow for the following applications:

1 **Organizational differentiation**: the ranking, by a multiple set of criteria, of students according to the value system of the school.
2 **Knowledge differentiation**: the selection and stratification by a multiple set of criteria, of knowledge made available to students by teachers according to the value system of the school.
3 **Subcultural polarization**: the formation of subcultures or 'group perspectives' (Woods, 1979) supportive of, or disaffected from, the dominant normative school culture.
4 **Knowledge culture polarization**: the formation of subcultures supportive of, or disaffected from, a particular knowledge-system culture.

My research explored how these differentiation and polarization processes were associated with gender and social class. The research was not designed to study these processes in a rigid mechanical way. Rather the concepts of differentiation and polarization gave the research an organizing framework and focus.

The concept of polarization was chosen in preference to resistance for two reasons. First, polarization describes a social process which affects pupils who are both pro- and anti- the school and I wanted to study both. Secondly, given the controversies and definitional difficulties over the resistance paradigm (Chapter 2), it is more methodologically sound to identify polarization in the first instance. This allows the anti-school pupils to be defined as either resistors or recusants. Having identified some polarization processes it is then possible, given further consideration, to judge whether or not such polarization also constituted resistance.

The School

Throughout this book pseudonyms are used to refer to the school and all the teachers and pupils. The fieldwork in the school, which will be known as Greenfield Comprehensive was conducted during 1986.

To study the processes of differentiation and polarization in a comprehensive I selected a school that was mixed-sex and had a broad spectrum of 'academic ability' and social class. I chose a comprehensive streamed by setting since this provided the most valuable data regarding debates about the generalizability of the differentiation–polarization theory. Setting is a more refined form of differentiation than streaming into forms or bands since pupils are ranked into different *subject* classes. In effect, setting is streaming within subjects. In principle, a pupil might be in the top set for English but the bottom set in mathematics. It is important to give careful consideration to this form of differentiation (hitherto fairly neglected in the research literature) in comprehensive schools because it could be argued that it offsets many of the related forms of polarization due to other types of streaming as documented by Lacey (1970), Hargreaves (1967), Woods (1979) and Ball (1981).

Greenfield is a large academically 'prestigious' comprehensive in a conurbation in the South of England. Approximately 1300 pupils (about half boys, half girls) attended the school which had a catchment area extending beyond the main conurbation to neighbouring small towns. Greenfield differed from the schools researched by Fuller (1980), Furlong (1984), Mac an Ghaill (1988) and Yates (1980) because almost all of the pupils were white and English. Consequently, unlike their research, neither racial nor ethnic differences were significant factors. A consequence and cause of the school's 'prestige' was that parents pressed to get their children enrolled there. Arguably, this partly explains why the educationally conscious professional middle classes were well represented in the school. A related factor is that the headteacher greatly valued good examination results. The head of department for each subject would be called to account for the relevant examination results at the end of each year. For this reason the school may be characterized as a fairly pressured academic environment. The teachers also placed a considerable amount of importance on school uniform which extended to schoolbags as well as clothes. Wearing the clothes was compulsory and strictly enforced, but the schoolbags were optional.

The campus was extensive with several playing fields and a swimming pool. The school catered for pupils from age 11–18 and divided into a lower and an upper section. The latter comprised the fourth to sixth years only. Thus there was a physical, as well as an intellectual, transition on entering the large fourth year.

The headteacher and deputy headteacher saw themselves as working in a 'progressive' school. Up to a point there was some truth in that perspective. For example, before beginning the first year prospective pupils would be asked about their friends who might be joining the school and, as far as possible, first-year classes would be organized around pupil friendships. Hence, in the first year pupils were organized into 'mixed-ability' classes, but from the second year and thereafter they were streamed into sets. Setting was based on the pupils' performance on 'cognitive ability tests' (CATs) usually administered in the first year together with teachers' reports on the pupils' abilities in each subject.

Another progressive movement in the school had been a significant discussion amongst the staff about equal opportunities for boys and girls. I was reminded of this on many occasions during my time in the school. However, the popularity of the equal-opportunities discussion had apparently waned two years prior to my research. The implication of this progressiveness for methodology is that insofar as the empirical research results are generalizable to other schools we can tentatively predict how results might be different in schools which are deemed to be more, or less, progressive in these respects.

The Sample

Most of the previous evidence and debates concerning differentiation and polarization has focused on the first four years of secondary schooling and I wanted to maintain this focus since I was also concerned with these processes. Given the length of the fieldwork I was unable to study, by participant observation, the actual movement through the school of a cohort of second-year pupils to their fourth year. For these reasons I chose a sample of fourth-year pupils so that I could analyse their historical records as well as their current social contexts and orientations.

I also wanted to study the pupils' perspectives on school knowledge and so it was important that my research paid considerable attention to the subject-option process. Given this I wanted the pupils to be able to recall the process as a past event so that they could, for example, inform me of any changes in their future expectations since making the options. Since the full range of options became available at the end of the third year this was another reason for choosing fourth years. Furthermore, and a point which is often overlooked, the option process does not end until a few weeks into the fourth year because some pupils want to change their options after trying a subject at the beginning of the fourth year.

In the fourth year there were some 300 pupils, all of whom studied English and mathematics. A large proportion also opted to study French. The fourth year included five English and five mathematics sets (E1 and M1 being the top sets for each subject and E5 and M5 the bottom) and two French sets (F1 and F2). English and mathematics classes were chosen for the research sample because those subjects were accorded high academic status and, therefore, reflected most strongly the school's evaluation of a pupil's overall academic ranking; and because they were compulsory in the fourth year with the consequence that membership of those classes was not biased towards a particular subject option and spanned the greatest range of 'ability'. French was chosen because, although no arts or modern-language subjects were compulsory in the fourth year it was compulsory to opt for one of the 'pure' sciences, biology, chemistry, or physics. This reflected the high status given to science within the school. Building French classes into the sample helped to balance the arts–science orientations within the sample. French was an appropriate subject for this task because, like the 'pure' sciences it was a mainstream academic subject.

To obtain the largest 'ability' range within subjects I took as my sample a top, middle and bottom set in English and mathematics (i.e., E1, E3, E5, M1, M3, and M5) and two French sets (F1 and F2). Due to overlaps in membership of the eight classes they included only 145 pupils (fifty-six boys and eighty-nine girls, average age 15 years), even though on average there were 27.5 pupils per class. The 'lowest ability' pupils tended not to opt for French sometimes on the advice of the school staff. As it was an option less pupils followed French than English or maths and the full range of 'ability' in French was accommodated by just two sets. F1 was the top set and F2 was the lower set which may be thought of as more comparable to the middle, rather than the bottom, sets of English and mathematics.

This gave me a total of eight 'sites' of empirical study (as shown below) each having a 1–1 correspondence with a class of pupils.

Sets	Maths	English	French
• Top (Set 1)	M1	E1	F1
• Middle (Set 2 or Set 3)	M3	E3	F2
• Bottom (Set 5)	M5	E5	

The sample consisted of considerably more girls than boys as a result of selecting these particular sets. A study of some of the intervening sets such as E4 and M4 instead of E3 and M3 would have reduced the proportion of girls in the sample but would not have provided me with such a breadth of differences in ability rankings — a more crucial part of the research design than obtaining an equal number of boys and girls. In fact, due to pupil absenteeism, only 127 of these pupils (fifty-two boys and seventy-five girls) completed all questionnaires. Most of my discussion is concerned with those 127 pupils about whom I collected the most data, though when considering longitudinal trends a further four pupils who did not attend the school for most of the four years are also omitted.

Research Methods

My approach followed in the tradition of ethnographic case-study research. One advantage of ethnography is that it employs multiple data sources, utilizing both quantitative and qualitative techniques as appropriate. to the research purpose and object (Hammersley and Atkinson, 1983). As recommended by Blackstone (1976), I applied a combination of research methods, including conventional questionnaires, intensive depth interviewing, and participant observation in the classroom.

After several weeks of classroom observation I administered questionnaires to the pupils including questions about friendships and dislikes, subjects followed, subject preferences, and career expectations. The pupils were also asked to write further about any aspect of the questionnaire if they desired. They were asked to complete it within one whole lesson (about forty-five minutes) without discussion. Most pupils managed to do this and I supervised the pupils, helping them with any problems of interpretation of questions.

In the classroom I used non-participant and participant observation techniques. For non-participant observation I used desk plans together with a considerably modified version of Flanders' (1970, p. 34) 'Interaction Analysis Category System'. Interactions were divided into those 'initiated' by the teacher and those 'initiated' by the pupils. Recording these required intense concentration and during such recording no form of participation in the class's activities was possible. I included non-verbal rebukes such as the teachers' use of their eyes or clicking of fingers followed by pointing in the category 'rebukes'. As Robertson (1981, p. 16) notes, teacher eye contact is 'particularly important in the communication of power and preference' but, of course, as Robertson also says 'a reliable interpretation of eye contact is only possible if given wider information about other relevant behaviour and the context in which it occurs'.

I do not suggest that conclusions should be drawn from this type of data alone. On the contrary, such data has considerable limitations and I found it useful merely as a crude indicator of classroom interaction. As Stubbs and Delamont (1976) argue, the Flanders Interaction Category system tends to ignore qualitative dimensions such as teacher styles and the importance of the actors' interpretations of the measured events. Also, they point out that Flanders' system is designed for classifying *interaction* delivered as public talk involving more than one person. Thus, it is not very suitable for lessons where one person reads aloud or lectures the whole time, or in classes where the pupils do a lot of silent seat-work or practical work singly or in groups and where public talk is limited.

My own interaction-analysis system also suffered from some of these problems in some classes, especially in the top mathematics set where there was very little public talk. Also, the top English set sometimes worked in groups as did the top French set. However, splitting into groupwork usually occurred nearly halfway into the lessons and my strategy was to record interactions only for the first twenty-five minutes of the lessons and then engage in *participant* observation.

My participant observation involved sitting with groups of the pupils during the lesson and asking them about their work or perhaps a previous incident in the lesson. Also, I would follow some pupils from one lesson to the next and generally try to get to know the pupils' thoughts about school life. I also took away samples of the pupils' work as well as teaching materials such as textbooks. The school records of the pupils in the eight classes were also examined.

Finally, all the eight teachers whom I had observed and twenty-six of the pupils were interviewed in depth in addition to my informal interactions with them during the fieldwork. The teacher interviews ranged from forty minutes to two hours in duration. Each teacher interview comprised questions designed to elucidate the 'gender profile' of the teacher, and to discuss the pupils in the observation class and the curriculum materials used. The pupil interviews ranged from twenty-five minutes to one-and-a-half hours in duration. The pupils for interview were selected so that there was approximately an equal number of boys and girls, and so that there was a fairly equal representation of pupils from each rank of sets (i.e., top, middle and bottom). The pupil interviews were designed to: elicit a full account of the reasons for their subject options; explore further subcultural friendship patterns; and focus on the ways in which streaming, social class and gender had influenced their responses to the school as an institution.

Chapter 4

Organizational Differentiation and Polarization: Setting, Social Class and Pupil Values

In this chapter I explore the elements of organizational differentiation associated with setting and related processes of subcultural polarization. This enables us to address Quine's criticisms of the differentiation–polarization theory mentioned in Chapter 2. If Quine is correct, then we would not expect to find any convincing positive relationship between academic performance and behaviour at Greenfield Comprehensive. If the theory is incorrect it follows that when pupils move from an undifferentiated situation in one period of time to a differentiated situation immediately afterwards there would be no reason to expect that they should exhibit a corresponding change in polarization. Furthermore, we would not expect any convincing positive relationship between subcultural friendship patterns in the pupil population and *either* differentiation *or* pro–anti-school value systems.

In studying organizational differentiation and subcultural polarization, therefore, my key strategy was to compare the differences over time in the academic performance and behaviour of pupils of contrasting ranking within the setting system. I do not make any grand claims to having established the correlation between social class and streaming since that has been well established by previous research (Floud and Halsey, 1957; Douglas, 1964; Holly, 1965; Ball, 1981). However, because we are particularly interested in the social-class implications of organizational differentiation it is desirable to establish that the sample is not idiosyncratic regarding the distribution of social classes across the streamed sets. To do this I first had to develop a measure of set ranking attributable to each pupil. This is not a trivial matter because, unlike bands and forms, sets do not immediately indicate the academic ranking of a pupil within the school. By itself, membership of a set only indicates the academic ranking of a pupil within a particular subject.

Table 1a: *Distribution of pupils in sets*

	Mathematics Sets					
English Sets	1	2	3	4	5	Totals
1	33	5	2	1	0	41
2	9	5	5	1	3	23
3	1	7	10	12	2	32
4	0	0	6	3	5	14
5	0	0	2	2	13	17
Totals	43	17	25	19	23	127

Table 1b: *Distribution of pupils in sets*

	Set-score on English 'plus' Mathematics (S[2])									
French Sets	2	3	4	5	6	7	8	9	10	Totals
1	28	8	5	3	2	2	1	0	0	49
2	2	2	3	2	3	7	2	0	3	24
No French	3	4	0	8	6	12	4	7	10	54
Totals	33	14	8	13	11	21	7	7	13	127

The Rigidity of Sets and the Set-score Indicator

In principle, setting allows for pupils to be in the top set for one subject and the bottom set for another. That is, it allows for 'mixed-ability' experiences for each pupil although only between classes and not necessarily within them. However, as shown in tables 1a and 1b, I found that to a large degree the same pupils were in the same rank of sets (i.e., top, middle, and bottom) across the English, mathematics and French classes. To be precise, out of the whole sample, only twelve pupils (9.4 per cent) were found in mathematics and English sets whose ranking differed by more than one.

A similar rigidity of sets was found to hold between mathematics and French, and English and French. This finding can be summarized by showing the association between the ranking of French sets and the aggregate set-score of each pupil for English and mathematics. Hence, the latter is an indicator of a pupil's ranking within the setting system based on the *two* subjects English and mathematics and I shall call it the Set-score indicator (S[2]). A pupil in E2 and M3, thus, has an S[2] of five.[1]

Table 1b shows that, for the seventy-three pupils in the sample who opted to study French, S[2] is clearly correlated with the ranking of the French sets. Of the forty-nine pupils who were in a top French set thirty-six (73.5 per cent) were also in at least one top English or mathematics set plus a second from top English or mathematics set. By contrast, the comparable figure for the twenty-four pupils in set F2 is 16.7 per cent.

Although this association is certainly marked it is not as strong as that between the mathematics and English sets. This is because F2 is not a bottom set in the same sense as E5 and M5. As French is an option, pupils who are thought to be weak at the subject are strongly advised not to opt to study it in the fourth form. Hence F2 functions more as a middle set than a bottom set. This explains why most of the pupils in F2 are found in the middling range of S[2] = 4 to 8.

Given the demonstrated rigidity of setting between English, mathematics and French it is justifiable to use S[2] as an indicator of the pupils' rankings within the setting system for academic subjects especially on the assumption that the major academic subjects of English, mathematics and French reflect most strongly the school's evaluation of a pupil's overall academic performance. Using S[2], the breakdown of the sample is as follows: twenty-eight boys and twenty-seven girls in the top range (S[2] = 2–4); ten boys and thirty-five girls in the middle range (S[2] = 5–7); fourteen boys and thirteen girls in the bottom range (S[2] = 8–10).

Setting and Social Class

School records were used to establish the social class of pupils. Notwithstanding controversies over social-class definitions (Acker, 1973; Goldthorpe and Payne, 1986), the occupation of the father was taken as the indicator of social class by use of the Registrar General's categorization of occupations into social-class groupings I–V. In fact, only sixty-one pupils (48 per cent) out of the sample could be ascribed a social class by this method due to incompleteness of records, father's unemployment or in some cases lack of father. Furthermore, the incompleteness of records in this regard was much more prevalent for pupils in the middle and bottom sets. In conjunction with previous research, this suggests that the social class of pupils from manual backgrounds tends to be under-reported to the school.

Working with this subsample, it is clear from Tables 2a and 2b that the non-manual social-class groupings (I, II and IIIN) are highly correlated with the low S[2] scores and hence the top sets. For example, of the fifteen pupils in social class I, none had an S[2] > 4. It is equally clear that the manual social-class groupings (IIIM, IV and V) are highly correlated with high S[2] scores and, hence, the middle and bottom sets. For example, of the eighteen pupils from manual skilled and unskilled social-class groupings, sixteen had S[2] > 4.

Teacher Differentiation: 'Academic Performance' and 'Behaviour'

The intelligibility of organizational differentiation as a process depends on the assumption that there is a positive relationship between academic

Table 2a: The number of pupils in each S[2] group distributed across social-class groupings

Social class	S[2]									
	2	3	4	5	6	7	8	9	10	Totals
I	11	2	2	0	0	0	0	0	0	15
II	8	4	1	2	0	3	0	1	0	19
IIIN	2	2	0	1	1	0	0	1	2	9
IIIM	1	0	1	1	2	3	3	2	2	15
IV	0	0	0	0	0	1	0	0	1	2
V	0	0	0	0	0	0	0	0	1	1
Totals	22	8	4	4	3	7	3	4	6	61

Table 2b: The number of pupils in broad social-class groupings distributed across broad S[2] ranges

Social class	S[2]			
	2–4	5–7	8–10	Totals
Non-manual	32	7	4	43
Manual	2	7	9	18
Totals	34	14	13	61

performance and 'behaviour' (Lacey, 1970, p. 82). This is because the normative value system of the school comprises behavioural and academic elements. The notion of organizational differentiation would become implausible if these elements were not positively related because a multiple set of *rankings* as well as criteria for ranking would be implied. The concept only makes sense if academic performance and 'behaviour' are positively related because they then converge on to the *same* ranking system.

To elaborate, the assumption is that 'behaviour' affects academic performance and vice versa because good behaviour involves paying attention to the teacher; and the teacher tends to become favourably disposed towards a pupil who is well behaved. In order to examine the plausibility of the assumption that teachers differentiate between pupils by a ranking system in which 'academic performance' and 'behaviour' converge, the teachers of each of the eight sets were asked to rank the pupils in their respective classes on descending scales of 1 to 10 on 'academic performance' and 1 to 5 on 'behaviour'. For 'academic performance' this was a fairly straightforward request since teachers were instructed that the scale should reflect the (then) GCE and CSE standards — since superseded by GCSE.

The definition of, and scale for, 'behaviour' was more problematic. I tried to impose a definition of 'behaviour' on the teachers to maximize uniformity. For the purposes of my research their assessment of 'behaviour' was to include 'attentiveness–disruptiveness', 'interest–apathy', 'effort–disobedience' and 'motivation'. Discussions with teachers about the behaviour indicator before they used it suggested that their first thought

Table 3: Teachers' assessments of pupils' 'academic performance' and 'behaviour' with S[2] ranges

	S[2] = 2–4 Estimated Behaviour				
Performance	Good	Medium	Bad	Totals	
Good	10	5	1	16	
Medium	10	3	5	18	
Bad	12	1	8	21	
Totals	32	9	14	55	Gamma = 0.12

	S[2] = 5–7 Estimated Behaviour				
Performance	Good	Medium	Bad	Totals	
Good	8	3	0	11	
Medium	6	6	3	15	
Bad	3	9	7	19	
Totals	17	18	10	45	Gamma = 0.64

	S[2] = 8–10 Estimated Behaviour				
Performance	Good	Medium	Bad	Totals	
Good	4	2	0	6	
Medium	4	4	3	11	
Bad	1	3	6	10	
Totals	9	9	9	27	Gamma = 0.69

in relation to grading behaviour was in terms of whether or not the pupils were 'discipline problems'. The scale ran as follows: 1 = good, 2 = fairly good, 3 = average, 4 = poor, and 5 = bad.

The grades of 'academic performance' and 'behaviour' were calculated separately for each pupil. The number of grades on each scale received by a pupil equalled the number of classes observed to which he or she belonged. For example, if a pupil was in E3, M3 and F2 — all classes which I observed — he or she received three grades on 'academic performance' and 'behaviour', one from each subject teacher. If pupils received more than one grade on either scale (as most did) then the arithmetic mean of their grades was calculated. The pupils were divided into three S[2] ranges (Table 3) and the pupils in each range were then ranked separately for 'academic performance' and 'behaviour' according to their calculated (mean) grades. Again separately for 'academic performance' and 'behaviour', the pupils were divided into three groups of approximately equal size. The group into which a pupil was placed depended on his or her ranking on 'academic performance' or 'behaviour' *within* the ranges.

The advantage of this method over examining teachers' records of pupils is that each teacher is asked to assess the pupils in a similar way. On the other hand, there are limitations to this because of the teachers' different interpretations of the 'behaviour' scale. Only three teachers used the full extent of this scale; one teacher used 1–4, three teachers confined themselves to 1–2 and one teacher used only grade 1 for his whole set.

Nevertheless, caveats aside, the results in Table 3 support the convergent relationship, primarily *within* sets. The statistic gamma (which varies from minus one to plus one) was used to describe this relationship precisely. In particular, it is significant that only one pupil in the whole sample who was considered to be 'badly behaved' was also a 'good performer'. However, the association between 'academic performance' and 'behaviour' is a weak one for the top S[2] range. This is partly explained by the large number of pupils in this range scoring very highly and densely on the 'behaviour' scale. Consequently well over half the number of pupils in this range fell into the 'good-behaviour' category. These results for the top S[2] range are not necessarily at odds with the positive relationship; they can be explained by acknowledging that differentiation is not so significant within the top sets. In fact, this finding supports previous research which has reported a similar trend for streamed forms (Lacey, 1970, p. 84).

Despite my guidelines the teachers' assessments of academic performance and behaviour are likely to have been affected by other factors associated with gender differences and perhaps girls' 'appropriation of femininity' (Anyon, 1983). In particular, Stanworth (1981) has reported that the performance of girls may be consistently underestimated because they are more quiet than 'dominant' boys in class. This could have implications for the results in Table 3 since there is not an equal number of boys and girls in each S[2] range. It might be argued, for example, that the middle-range scores for academic performance are likely to be relatively low because of the large proportion of girls with S[2] = 5–7. On the other hand, those classes with large proportions of girls also contain fewer dominant boys. Indeed, my classroom observation suggested that the girls tended to be more outspoken when in the majority.

Teachers' estimates of 'behaviour' also have complex gender dimensions. Some teachers clearly felt that boys were, on the whole, more likely to cause discipline problems than girls. One teacher frequently used the well-known threat: 'I'll make you sit with the girls', in order to try to discipline troublesome boys. The perceptions of these teachers are consistent with research which claims that boys gain greater attention because 'they cause more trouble for the teacher' (Riddell, 1992). However, Davies (1983) argues that adolescent girls tend to be more concerned about their self-presentation and image in the classroom than boys, and that this can give rise to considerable resistance to school uniform. I witnessed many occasions on which girls were 'ticked off' in class because they were not wearing the correct uniform but only two for boys. It is difficult, therefore, to assess the precise quantitative impact sex differences might have on the 'behaviour' estimates. However, most significantly the trends and correlations shown in Table 3 also held when the scores for boys and girls were analysed separately. This implies that, although gender differentiation by teachers is evident, there remains a 'behaviour'–performance correlation which is independent of sex.

Underlying the data presented in Table 3 is the fact that, without exception, the scores which defined the lower bounds of the categories 'good', 'medium' and 'bad' for both 'academic performance' and 'behaviour' were set highest for the highest S[2] range and lowest for the lowest S[2] range. This implies that the positive relationship holds *between* sets also. More direct, but non-quantitative, evidence of this can be seen by considering how teachers stereotype sets. The following three examples illustrate the point:

M1 teacher: You don't find any behaviour problems with the top set — they've got the intelligence.

M5 teacher: When you get your next year's timetable and you see that it is a top or bottom set then you get certain images. If you get a top set you tend to think that their behaviour will be better. You tend to think with a bottom set you will get more discipline problems. I look forward to teaching my top-set third year but dread my bottom-set third year. With the bottom group I go in with a stony face but I know that with the top set if I say fun's over they will stop. But if I give a bottom set rope they'll take advantage of you.

E5 teacher: Take the high-achieving girls. They conform in terms of uniform. They work hard. They seem to have internalized the norms of the school in terms of response to teachers in every way. Then there are the low achievers. They don't appear to conform in terms of dress. They get into trouble with teachers. Their response to teachers' interjections is often fairly hostile. They don't accept the system, they fight it.

It is important to emphasize that these comments do not relate to some *specific* cohort of pupils. Instead they relate to *general ideas* which label pupils and, therefore, should be understood as a way of stereotyping rather than as assessments based on some particular empirical reality. As Allport (1954) explains, using the term 'Negro' as an illustration:

a stereotype is not identical with a category; it is a fixed idea that accompanies a category. . . . Stereotype enters in when, and if, the initial category is freighted with pictures and judgements of the Negro as musical, lazy, superstitious or what not. The stereotype is not in itself the core of the concept. It operates however in such a way as to prevent differentiated thinking about the concept (Allport, 1954, p. 187).

For example, the teacher of M5 made judgments about the likely behaviour of sets of pupils before meeting any of them. For these reasons it cannot be plausibly argued, for instance, that these teachers are simply making informed judgments about pupils on the basis of their IQs or some particular mischievous tendencies. Insofar as teachers use stereotypes of sets to make empirical extrapolations they are differentiating between pupils' behaviour on the basis of set-ranking rather than pupils' actual behaviour.

This kind of differentiation between sets is also evident in the teachers' responses to deviance in the classroom. Consider the following examples from my lesson notes:

Lesson notes for French set 1
The lesson is devoted to revising the future tense. The teacher writes verbs and verb endings on the board and the pupils are quiet and attentive. They take down the work diligently . . . The teacher rebukes Andrew by saying: 'Andrew, why are we playing with a calculator. Is it a French calculator?' The teacher says this in a tired and sarcastic way. Andrew stops his fiddling.

Lesson notes for French set 2
The class is reading (by translation) through passages in their French textbook. Alan mutters a rude comment about the lesson to his friends, who start laughing. The teacher says 'Alan, what did you say? Share it with the rest of the class'. Alan replies 'I didn't say anything'. Teacher now shouting and pointing 'Alan, what did you say?' No response. Teacher shouts 'Right, work centre (pointing to the door), I've got no time for you here'.

Andrew's rebuke in F1 was one of the few I observed while in that class. In that context it can be thought of as a fairly major ticking off of a pupil for that set. Also, the weary and sarcastic way that the rebuke was delivered implied that Andrew was letting down the rest of the class as well as the teacher. The teacher was able to present confidently Andrew's fiddling as an undesirable nuisance to the whole class. Andrew was said to be 'playing', implying a kind of 'immaturity' which violated the 'sensible' attitude to school work expected of the top set. By contrast, Alan's rude remark about the lesson was given support and positive recognition by others in the class by their laughing. The teacher was not able to present his behaviour as contrary to the norms of the class and saw it as an immediate threat to his authority. A major rebuke for F2 was a dismissal to the 'work centre', which was a kind of detention centre, supervised by a teacher, for pupils who misbehaved during school hours. It was one of the most severe sanctions a classroom teacher could impose on a pupil. During all my time at the school I found no one from the top sets who had ever been sent to the 'work centre'. Yet I observed this on many occasions in the middle and bottom sets.

Thus, teachers identified the top sets with norms of good behaviour and the middle and lower sets with norms of bad behaviour. Moreover, the immediacy of the teachers' experiences with setted classes tended to reinforce their expectations about individual pupils' behavioural characteristics, and to underplay the significance of underlying organizational factors in producing those experiences.

Polarization: 'Academic Performance' and 'Behaviour'

Evidently setting in Greenfield contributed to organizational differentiation of a kind similar to that discussed by Lacey (1970) and Hargreaves (1967) and Ball (1981). If the setting in the school were associated with polarization then we would expect to find the development of anti-school and pro-school subcultures amongst the pupils. Furthermore, we would expect the former to be dominated by pupils from the lower sets with less commitment to academic work and the behavioural rules of the school and the latter to be dominated by pupils from the top sets with considerable commitment to school tasks and the school's behavioural norms. I wanted to see if subcultures with these characteristics developed most strikingly from the end of the first year when 'mixed-ability' classes were replaced by streamed sets. I constructed several indicators to examine this scenario.

One commonly used indicator of the effort pupils devote to school tasks is the amount of time they spend on homework (Natriello and McDill, 1986). The pupils were asked to estimate the amount of time they spent on their mathematics and English homeworks per week. These two subjects were chosen to control for subject variation since all fourth-year pupils took English and mathematics. The results shown in Tables 4a and 4b indicate a considerable trend in support of the idea that pupils in the top sets adopted pro-school values much more than pupils in the lower sets. The top S[2] range consistently peaks at 2–3 hours for homework time on each subject whilst all but one of the other S[2] ranges peak at less than this. It is also significant that only two out of fifty-five pupils in the top S[2] range spent less than half an hour on English or mathematics (no one spending less than half an hour on both) whilst this was the case for ten

Table 4a: *Time spent on English homework per week*

S[2]				Hours spent			
	< $\frac{1}{2}$	$\frac{1}{2}$–1	1–2	2–3	3–4	>4	Totals
2–4	0	5	20	29	1	0	55
5–7	1	3	22	13	5	1	45
8–10	3	6	10	6	2	0	27
Totals	4	14	52	48	8	1	127

Table 4b: *Time spent on Mathematics homework per week*

S[2]				Hours spent			
	< $\frac{1}{2}$	$\frac{1}{2}$–1	1–2	2–3	3–4	>4	Totals
2–4	2	2	18	27	6	0	55
5–7	5	4	10	20	5	1	45
8–10	4	9	8	2	3	1	27
Totals	11	15	36	49	14	2	127

out of seventy-two pupils in the other S[2] ranges, three of whom spent less than half an hour on both.

Nevertheless these data are limited. It could be argued that they are specific to mathematics and English and, further, that they reflect the pupils' current commitment to homework rather than a more long-term and lasting phenomenon. One further objection might be that these homework data do not reflect *solely* commitment because pupils in bottom and middle sets may not have been *given* the same potential load of homework by the teacher in the first place. For these reasons I sought a better and supplementary indicator which applied to all subjects over time and which related to *missed* schoolwork.

To do this I consulted school records. These included teachers' reports of assignments missed by each pupil. Unfortunately I was unable to examine four pupil records because staff were using them during my fieldwork. In addition, four pupils in the sample had not attended the school for most of the four years. Consequently, the reported missed assignments (m.a.s) of only 119 pupils in the sample were analysed. Over the four years at Greenfield, pupils from the fourth-year middle and bottom S[2] ranges were found to receive many more m.a.s than fourth-year pupils from the top S[2] range (Table 5).[2] In addition, on average, only 36.5 per cent of the top S[2] range pupils received any m.a.s at all, whilst the comparable figures for the middle and bottom ranges were 63 per cent and 97 per cent respectively. It is important to distinguish between the assignments which pupils actually missed and missed assignment *reports* (m.a.s). Many missed assignments can go unreported, because either they are not brought to a teacher's attention or the teacher uses his or her discretion not to report. Secondly, m.a.s tend to refer to several uncompleted tasks and they usually relate to a teacher's serious concern over a

Table 5: *Number of missed assignment reports received (n[m.a.])*

		Years				
S[2]	No. of pupils	1st	2nd	3rd	4th	Totals
2	32	1(0.03)	0(0.0)	2(0.06)	5(0.16)	10(0.3)
3	12	1(0.08)	0(0.0)	9(0.75)	10(0.83)	21(1.75)
4	8	0(0.0)	1(0.13)	10(1.25)	6(0.75)	19(2.38)
5	12	1(0.08)	3(0.25)	9(0.75)	17(1.42)	40(3.33)
6	11	0(0)	2(0.2)	5(0.4)	7(0.7)	14(1.3)
7	17	1(0.06)	4(0.22)	10(0.55)	8(0.47)	25(1.47)
8	7	2(0.29)	7(1.0)	9(1.29)	6(0.86)	26(3.71)
9	7	5(0.71)	1(0.14)	7(1.0)	24(3.43)	37(5.28)
10	13	1(0.1)	6(0.5)	6(0.7)	24(2.4)	39(3.9)
Totals	119	12(0.1)	24(0.2)	67(0.55)	107(0.87)	231(1.89)

Note: Bracketed numbers are the number of missed-assignment notes received per pupil of that S[2] score.

pupil's efforts and performance. They are *not* a documentation of each and every task uncompleted by a pupil.

Teachers also regularly reported on the pupils' 'behaviour'. As a result school records included documentation of 'bad behaviour' notes (b.b.s). As with m.a.s, b.b.s were not given lightly. They represented a much more serious ticking off of a pupil than a rebuke in class. They were the most serious sanction a teacher could bring to bear on a pupil on behavioural grounds short of sending the pupil to the 'work centre' or reporting a pupil directly to the deputy headteacher. A b.b. contained the following options for the reporting teacher to tick plus a space to write any alternative or additional information:

- abusive to teacher;
- violent to other pupils;
- consistently talking in class;
- deliberately disruptive in class;
- absent from class;
- late to lesson;
- refusal to work in class;
- damage to school property; and
- did not arrive for my detention.

Like m.a.s, b.b.s were received mostly by pupils in the middle and bottom sets. Furthermore, these pupils received many more b.b.s on average than pupils in the top sets did (Table 6).

Careful examination of Tables 7a and 7b reveals that during the unstreamed first year there were no appreciable quantitative differences (as measured in absolute terms or as proportions) between the pupils who would later comprise the top S[2] < 5 range and those who would later make up the middle S[2] = 5–7 range. However, by the end of the second

Table 6:   Number of 'bad behaviour' notes received (n[b.b.])

S[2]	No. of pupils	Years				
		1st	2nd	3rd	4th	Totals
2	32	3(0.09)	12(0.38)	23(0.72)	25(0.78)	63(1.97)
3	12	4(0.33)	15(1.25)	16(1.33)	14(1.17)	49(4.08)
4	8	1(0.13)	3(0.38)	10(1.25)	10(1.25)	24(3.0)
5	12	4(0.33)	29(2.42)	21(1.75)	20(1.67)	74(6.17)
6	11	0(0.0)	2(0.2)	7(0.64)	14(1.4)	24(2.18)
7	17	2(0.11)	20(1.18)	32(1.88)	24(1.41)	82(4.82)
8	7	3(0.43)	8(1.14)	64(9.14)	43(6.14)	139(19.9)
9	7	11(1.57)	45(6.43)	76(10.86)	70(10.0)	206(29.4)
10	13	1(0.08)	25(1.92)	42(3.23)	54(4.15)	123(9.46)
Totals	119	29(0.24)	159(1.34)	291(2.45)	274(2.3)	784(6.59)

Note: Bracketed numbers are the number of 'bad behaviour' notes received per pupil of that S[2] score.

year very significant differences had emerged. The middle range received twice as many b.b.s per pupil and ten times as many m.a.s. per pupil. A large degree of polarization between these two ranges, therefore, can be attributed to the transition from the unstreamed first year to the setted second year.

Polarization is seen to decrease in the third and fourth years by comparison with the second year, but always remains greater than that in the first year. These results can be interpreted as an indication that inter-set differentiation is not the sole agent in creating pro- and anti-school values which give rise to polarization. In the fourth year within the middle sets there was a considerable split in values and this is likely to have been the case in the third year also. Indeed, during the third year, with the onset of increased examination/future career pressure we might expect a reinforcement of the pro-school values of some middle-set pupils more than counterbalancing the increases in anti-school values amongst other middle-set pupils and resulting in an overall suppression of the growth in n[m.a.] and n[b.b] moving from second to third year.[3]

This reduction in polarization in the third year also coincides with a sharp increase in n[m.a] and n[b.b] for the top range. That may be due to the increased academic pressure applied to these pupils in order to achieve a very high level of attainment in their third-year examinations. Under such conditions teachers' high expectations of the top sets might cause them to report more missed assignments and cases of 'bad' behaviour, thus increasing the amount of differentiation *within* the top sets. This hypothesis is supported by the fact that in the second year the numbers of missed assignment reports for each of S[2] = 2, 3 and 4 are equally negligible (0, 0 and 1 respectively), but in the third year n[m.a.] for S[2] = 3 and S[2] = 4 increase considerably to 9 and 10 respectively whilst for S[2] = 2 it increases to only 2.

In the fourth year the extent of organizational differentiation between

Table 7a: *Growth in number of missed assignment reports received*

			Years		
S[2]	No. of pupils	1st	2nd	3rd	4th
<5	52	2(0.04)	1(0.02)	21(0.4)	21(0.4)
5–7	40	2(0.05)	9(0.23)	24(0.6)	32(0.8)
Difference		0	8	3	11
Proportions of per pupil		1.25	11.5	1.5	2.0

Note: Bracketed numbers are the number of m.a.s received per pupil of that S[2] score.

Table 7b: *Growth in number of bad behaviour notes received*

			Years		
S[2]	No. of pupils	1st	2nd	3rd	4th
<5	52	8(0.15)	30(0.58)	49(0.94)	49(0.94)
5–7	40	6(0.15)	51(1.28)	60(1.5)	58(1.45)
Difference		2	21	11	9
Proportions of per pupil		1.0	2.2	1.6	1.5

Note: Bracketed numbers are the number of b.b.s received per pupils of that S[2] score.

these two ranges is likely to be slightly reduced due to the onset of subject options creating a greater overlap between the two ranges in some classes. Further, the differentiation within the top range is likely to be reduced as these pupils are able to discard the subjects they dislike the most and the ones at which they experience the greatest degree of failure. These processes in the fourth year probably explain the decrease in growth of the receipt of m.a.s and b.b.s for both ranges and the decrease in polarization between the ranges. But overall Tables 7a and 7b show strong evidence of polarization in the second year. For the pupils with S[2] < 8 polarization continues to exist in the third and fourth years although it is less marked than in the second year.

Comparing the pupils in the top sets with those in the bottom sets I found that there were significant quantitative differences between the two subsamples S[2] = 2 and S[2] > 7 in the receipt of b.b.s and m.a.s at the end of the first year (Tables 7c and 7d). However, during the years of streamed setting these differences were magnified in absolute terms very considerably. These two subsamples are of approximately equal size and, arguably, bring with them into the streamed sets established differences in 'behaviour' and commitment to schoolwork. Nevertheless, the growth of the absolute differences cannot be obviously explained by some inherent pupil predispositions which are independent of the streaming system. Unlike, that between the top and middle sets (Tables 7a and 7b), the polarization (as measured by absolute differences) between the top sets and the bottom sets *increases during the third and fourth years* (Tables 7c and 7d). The pressure of third-year examinations is felt less by the bottom sets than

Table 7c: *Growth in number of missed-assignment reports received*

S[2]	No. of pupils	1st	2nd	3rd	4th
			Years		
2	32	1	0[0]	2[1]	5[3]
8–10	27	8	14[9]	22[11]	54[14]
Difference		7	14	20	49
Proportions		8	I	11	10.8

Notes:
1 I equals infinity.
2 Square brackets indicate the number of pupils in that year who have increased their n[m.a.] since the previous year.

Table 7d: *Growth in number of 'bad-behaviour' notes received*

S[2]	No. of pupils	1st	2nd	3rd	4th
			Years		
2	32	3	12[6]	23[9]	25[9]
8–10	27	15	78[18]	182[20]	167[7]
Difference		12	66	159	142
Proportions		5	6.5	7.9	6.7

Note: Square brackets indicate the number of pupils in that year who have increased their n[b.b.] since the previous year.

the middle sets because their ranking puts any high academic achievement out of reach. Again unlike the middle sets, in the fourth year the bottom sets were not significantly divided, but predominantly anti-school.

If the differences in n[m.a.] and n[b.b] between the top and bottom sets are measured by proportions instead of in absolute terms, however, it might be argued that, although Table 7c shows clear evidence of a growth in polarization between the unstreamed first year and setted second year, all the other data could be explained by the reproduction (e.g., through maturation) of differences in pupil predispositions evident in the first year. That alternative argument implies that setting is not such a significant factor in creating the differences in n[m.a.] and n[b.b.] between the top and bottom sets, but rather that those differences are due to individually based inherent qualities of the particular pupils involved. But a closer examination of the evidence renders that alternative view at worst very implausible and at best very limited.

For example, Table 7c shows that in the setted second, third and fourth years 9, 11, and 14 bottom-set pupils respectively increased their receipt of m.a.s whereas the comparable figures regarding the top set pupils are 0, 1, and 3 respectively. Similarly, for Table 7d at least until the fourth year. However, Tables 7e and 7f show that only 5 or 6 pupils in the bottom sets could possibly be responsible for the n[m.a] and n[b.b.] figures in the first year which form the basis on which to calculate increases in polarization thereafter. In fact, in the case of m.a.s the five

Table 7e: *Number of m.a.s received by bottom-set pupils in first four years divided between those receiving m.a.s in the 1st year and those not*

		Years			
S[2]	No. of pupils	1st	2nd	3rd	4th
8–10	22	0	11	15	33
8–10	5	8	3	7	21

Table 7f: *Number of b.b.s received by bottom-set pupils in first four years divided between those receiving b.b.s in the 1st year and those not*

		Years			
S[2]	No. of pupils	1st	2nd	3rd	4th
8–10	21	0	31	98	104
8–10	6	15	47	84	63

pupils, that might be supposed to be different in predisposition from the top-set pupils, decline quite markedly in their receipt of m.a.s in the second and third years rather like the top-set pupils but unlike the other bottom-set pupils. This indicates that these pupils were not predisposed to the overall trends of the bottom set pupils regarding m.a.s. It is just possible that the 'bad behaviour' records of the 6 bottom-set pupils in the second row of Table 7f might be explained by pupil predispositions evident in the first year but it is certainly not possible to argue that case for the other 21 bottom-set pupils.

Overall, then, the longitudinal data in Tables 7a–f support the theory that a polarization associated with setting occurs amongst the pupil population, but with some qualifications concerning value divisions within the middle sets and the impact of some additional factors in the third and fourth years not taken account of by the tables themselves.[4] Evidently very significant polarization took place (whether measured by absolute differences or proportions) between the first and second years when the most central differentiation occurred with the onset of streaming by sets.

Given the very similar trends between S[2] and both the number of m.a.s and the number of b.b.s, one would expect the number of missed assignments received (n[m.a.]) and the number of 'bad behaviour' notes received (n[b.b.]) to be significantly and positively correlated. Of course, these trends do not guarantee such a correlation so I carried out an independent calculation and found that n[m.a.] and n[b.b.] are highly correlated ($r = 0.55$). Although girls were found to receive less m.a.s and less b.b.s *overall* than boys, the same *trends* as shown in Tables 5 and 6 (and similar correlations) were found for boys and girls when analysed separately. Hence, sex differences are not significant in accounting for the set-related polarization amongst the pupils. The overall sex differences could imply several different factors, but these indicators are not the best way of

Table 8: Correlation between missed assignments and 'bad-behaviour' notes

No. of 'bad behaviour' notes n[b.b.]	No. of missed assignments n[m.a.]		
	'good' 0–1	'medium' 2–5	'bad' >5
'good' 0–2	61 [S = 4.0]	7 [S = 7.1]	0 [no value]
'medium' 3–8	12 [S = 6.1]	14 [S = 6.5]	4 [S = 6.3]
'bad' >8	5 [S = 5.8]	9 [S = 7.3]	7 [S = 6.9]

Notes:
1 Gamma = 0.82.
2 S refers to the average S[2] score over the whole of each cell sample.

explaining such differences. For example, the fact that girls tend to receive less m.a.s than boys could imply that girls tend to be more conscientious. On the other hand, it could imply that teachers tend to expect less work from girls and, therefore, less frequently report girls for missing assignments than boys.

The significant correlation between n[m.a.] and n[b.b.] is highlighted by the interval representation in Table 8 which includes the average S[2] score of the subsample in each cell. The interval boundaries were chosen on the basis of my subjective understanding of the raw data. A pupil who received a maximum of only one m.a. and/or two b.b.s over four years was unquestionably *relatively* well behaved and/or committed to school-work according to the values of the school. However, a pupil who received more than five m.a.s and/or more than eight b.b.s was certainly *relatively* badly behaved and/or uncommitted to academic work according to the school's values. These results support the hypothesis that the prevalence of commitment to school work and school behavioural norms is related to organizational differentiation (indicated by the substantial difference in the average S[2] score of the top-left cell and its counterparts in the other cells) and, further, that the pupils who missed assignments were also those who breached the behavioural rules of the school (indicated by the value of r). However, it would be foolish to conclude that all the pupils in the 'good–good' category have pro-school attitudes because it reflects only the school's official record of pupils. Some of these pupils might simply manage to avoid being reported for actions deriving from anti-school attitudes.

Superficially the results in Table 8 might be thought to be consistent with an alternative individualistic 'pupil-deficit' hypothesis which excludes organizational differentiation as a causal mechanism. That is, that the 'less

Table 9: *Mean CAT stanine scores of pupils falling into categories of Table 8*

	n[m.a.]		
n[b.b.]	'good'	'medium'	'bad'
'good'	7.2(45)	5.8(7)	no value
'medium'	6.3(7)	6.7(12)	6.8(2)
'bad'	5.7(3)	5.2(7)	6.7(5)

Notes:
1 Bracketed numbers refer to the number of pupils in each cell sample for which CAT scores were available.
2 $r_{n[m.a.], n[b.b.]} = 0.52$
  $r_{n[m.a.], CAT} = -0.15$
  $r_{n[b.b.], CAT} = -0.26$
  $r_{n[m.a.], n[b.b.]/CAT} = 0.504$

able' pupils were placed in the lower sets and *because* of their 'lesser ability' they missed more school work and broke more of the school rules than the 'more able' pupils placed in the top sets. To examine the validity of this alternative interpretation of the results in Table 8 the pupils' scores on standardized 'Cognitive Abilities Tests' (CATs) were analysed (Thorndike and Hagen, 1973a; 1973b). I should emphasize that in utilizing 'cognitive-ability' test assessments I am not suggesting that such individualistic abstracted assessments should be accepted uncritically, or that ability should be naturalized (Chapter 1). Rather, I use them as heuristic devices to perform sociological comparisons.

According to the school records, only eighty-eight of the pupils had undergone directly comparable CATs. These tests involved measuring the pupils' 'ability' to perform certain 'verbal', 'non-verbal' and 'quantitative' tasks (Thorndike and Hagen, 1973a; 1973b). For each pupil the scores were converted to the standardized stanine scores (which range from 1 = very low to 9 = very high) using an appropriate table of norms (Thorndike and Hagen, 1973c, p. 28) and then an average of the three stanine scores was calculated thus yielding the CAT stanine (CAT st) for each pupil.

Considering Table 9, we may note that the maximum difference between the average CAT st scores for each cell is 2.0. It is also worth noting, at this point, that the CAT guidelines label 'average ability' as spanning from 4.0–6.0, also a difference of 2.0 (Thorndike and Hagen, 1973c, p. 28). This observation is at least suggestive that the correlation between the n[m.a.] and n[b.b.] cannot be explained to any significant degree by the pupils' CAT st. Furthermore, the correlations between n[m.a] and CAT st ($r_{n[m.a.], CAT}$), and n[b.b.] and CAT st ($r_{n[b.b.], CAT}$) for the eighty-eight pupils are only weakly negative. More precisely, the partial correlation between n[m.a.] and n[b.b.] controlling for CAT st ($r_{n[m.a.], n[b.b.]/CAT}$) = 0.504 is almost as significantly positive as the overall correlation between n[m.a.] and n[b.b] for these eighty-eight pupils ($r_{n[m.a.], n[b.b.]} = 0.52$).

Moreover, if one considers the diagonal of Table 9 for which the largest percentage samples of CAT st scores are available (45 out of 61 = 73.8 per cent, 12 out of 14 = 85.7 per cent, and 5 out of 7 = 71.4 per cent), it can be seen that there is no difference between the 'medium–medium' and the 'bad–bad' categories and only a 0.5 difference between either of these and the 'good–good' category. This suggests that there is no good reason to accept the hypothesis that CAT stanines significantly explain the variations in 'academic performance' and 'behaviour' represented in Table 8.

If the polarization in academic performance and 'behaviour' documented in the school records reflects polarization of pro- and anti-school values then we would expect to find those values to manifest themselves in the pupils' perspectives on school. Specifically we would expect most, if not all, of the seven pupils falling into the 'bad–bad' category in Table 9 to exhibit anti-school attitudes. We would also expect them to have been ranked either in the middle or bottom sets within the streaming system *or* possibly ranked at the bottom of the top sets. It is important to note that polarization into anti-school subcultures need not increase monotonically as one descends the ranking system. Ball (1981), for instance, found the greatest degree of anti-school values in the middle bands. This was because the middle-band pupils, more than the bottom-band pupils, felt that they were failing relative to the top-band pupils. Similarly, Lacey (1970) found that those pupils in the top form who were ranked at the very bottom of the form were also likely to develop anti-school attitudes because they felt failures relative to the rest of the form. Rather the question is whether organizational differentiation (between or within sets) is a major mechanism in producing anti-school and pro-school polarization.

For each of the seven 'bad–bad' pupils the number of 'bad-behaviour' notes received in the unstreamed first year ($n[b.b.]_{1st}$) was never more than the number received in the second, third or fourth years and, in fact, it was nearly always much less. Exactly the same point holds for m.a.s. These time-dependent data lend further support to the thesis that setting at Greenfield contributed to polarization since these pupils received a disproportionately large number of b.b.s and m.a.s during their three streamed years up to the end of fourth year as compared with their unstreamed first year.

The following static data on these pupils' attitudes in the late fourth year confirm the existence of anti-school polarization. The seven pupils were asked: 'Do you look forward to leaving school?' Six replied 'yes', giving the following reasons for their answers.

Pupil A $S[2] = 3$, $n[b.b.]_{1st} = 4$, $n[b.b.] = 36$, $n[m.a.]_{1st} = 1$, $n[m.a.] = 13$,
CAT: stanine = 8
Yes because when you're in school you're bossed around, stuck in uniform and they don't let you have any individuality.

Pupil B $S[2] = 5$, $n[b.b.]_{1st} = 1$, $n[b.b.] = 9$, $n[m.a.]_{1st} = 0$, $n[m.a.] = 12$,
CAT: stanine = 8.33
. . . because once you're out of school you get treated with respect.

Pupil C $S[2] = 5$, $n[b.b.]_{1st} = 0$, $n[b.b.] = 24$, $n[m.a.]_{1st} = 0$, $n[m.a.] = 7$,
CAT: stanine = 7.33
I hate school.

Pupil D $S[2] = 8$, $n[b.b.]_{1st} = 2$, $n[b.b.] = 23$, $n[m.a.]_{1st} = 2$, $n[m.a.] = 13$,
CAT: no record.
I want to go to art college.

Pupil E $S[2] = 9$, $n[b.b.]_{1st} = 2$, $n[b.b.] = 36$, $n[m.a.]_{1st} = 2$, $n[m.a.] = 11$,
CAT: stanine = 5
When you leave school you have something to look forward to.

Pupil F $S[2] = 10$, $n[b.b.]_{1st} = 1$, $n[b.b.] = 47$, $n[m.a.]_{1st} = 1$, $n[m.a.] = 7$,
CAT: stanine = 5
Get a job and leave home.

These comments reflect anti-school attitudes with the possible exceptions of those made by pupils D and F. Pupil D, however, received many rebukes in class and in a French class I observed that the teacher sent him to the 'work centre'. An interview with this pupil indicated that he disliked most school work, especially homework. Similarly, an interview with pupil F revealed that he was regularly sent to the 'work centre' and had been suspended from the school for 'bad behaviour'. He felt 'bossed around' at school and disliked many of his teachers. It can be reasonably concluded that pupils A–F have basically anti-school values.

Pupil A is the only member of the 'bad–bad' category from the top $S[2]$ range. However, his mathematics teacher gave him the lowest estimate of 'academic performance' in that class. This teacher used only the scores 1–3. Pupil A received a 3 whilst the rest of the class received a 1 or 2. In addition the teacher commented that Pupil A needed to be put into a lower mathematics set. Hence, a plausible explanation for Pupil A's anti-school values is *intra*-set, rather than inter-set, differentiation. The one pupil, G ($S[2] = 8$, $n[b.b.]_{1st} = 1$, $n[b.b.] = 27$, $n[m.a.]_{1st} = 0$, $n[m.a.] = 8$), who did not look forward to leaving school in the 'bad–bad' category felt that without school he would get bored but did not offer any positive comments about the school.

A sharp contrast can be drawn between these seven pupils and the sixty-two pupils falling into the 'good–good' category of Table 8. By definition the latter received, in total, no more than one m.a. and two b.b.s. Consequently, there is little or no difference between their 'bad behaviour' and 'missed-assignment' records for the unstreamed first and the streamed second, third and fourth years. This indicates the development, over time, of pro-school values.

Questionnaire data imply that most of the 'good–good' pupils did indeed hold pro-school attitudes. Of the sixty-two, 32 (51.6 per cent) did not look forward to leaving school, 25 (40.3 per cent) did and 5 (8.1 per cent) were unsure. Furthermore, by analysing the reasons given by the 25 pupils who did look forward to leaving school it was possible to judge that only 8 clearly held anti-school values (with an average S[2] score of 5), 8 clearly held pro-school values (with an average S[2] score of 4) and the other 9 (with an average S[2] score of 4.2) could not be clearly categorized. A few examples of reasons judged to imply anti-school values are given below.

So I can do what I want.
So I can start again — a new start.
I dislike school, I would like to have more freedom to do what I want.
I hate school, all my real friends are in jobs. I've lost interest.

For these pupils the school was inhibiting and undermining in absolute terms. By contrast, those pupils who looked forward to leaving school, but held pro-school values, tended to perceive school as only *relatively* worse than other future possibilities and valued their school work as a means to accessing better future options. For example:

I want to get a good steady job. I hope that all the work at school will help me do that.
I would like to go to university and specialize instead of doing eight subjects.
[Leaving school] will give me the opportunity to broaden my horizons, so to speak, travel and meet new people, and do a job that interests me.
I want to be able to get my exams over with and then plan my career.

Overall, then, as many as 64.5 per cent of the 'good–good' pupils tended towards pro-school values. Although reflected in static, rather than developmental, data, these pupil perspectives also lend support to the theory that polarization is associated with differentiation whereas the eight 'good–good' pupils with anti-school values do not. On the other hand, it might be possible to explain at least some of these eight anomalies within the theory. For instance four of these pupils were in lower or bottom sets and another one who had a S[2] score of 4 was ranked almost at the bottom of her top-set French class. Hence, it could be argued that for these five cases anti-school attitudes (and therefore polarization) did indeed arise out of differentiation, but without being recorded by the school in the form of m.a.s and b.b.s. It should be noted, however, that the data in Table 8 cannot be compromised in this way symmetrically; it is much less plausible to argue that the pupils falling into the 'bad–bad' category were really relatively better behaved and more committed to school assignments than the records indicate.

Polarization: Friendship Choices

One way of investigating whether the pro-school and anti-school values held by individual pupils reflect a subcultural polarization is to study their friendship patterns. This is based on the hypothesis that pupils of different ranks within the streaming system develop different concerns, and therefore values, in relation to the school. Furthermore, these values tend to be sustained through communication about common concerns and the development of friendships. Thus, if setting does give rise to polarization then there should be an identifiable association between setting and the structure of friendship patterns.

All the pupils in the sample were asked to list their six closest friends in the fourth year and also pupils in the school they particularly disliked/ could not get on with. Their responses were then subjected to sociometric analysis, taking separately the members of the eight classes I had been observing. Of course, I could only study friendship and enmity patterns *within* my sample if I was to avoid the pitfalls of abstracting the sociomatrices beyond classroom observation (Gronlund, 1959). Obviously requesting the pupils to limit themselves to friends and dislikes from the sample would have meant imposing an artificial boundary around their actual social relations, whereas the fourth year and the school were proper sociological groups since all members of the sample recognized, and belonged to, them.[5] Taking the fourth year as such a group also allowed me to see the extent to which members of the eight classes in the sample chose their friends from outside the sample.

Table 10 shows that just over a quarter of the friendship choices were to pupils outside the eight classes. More significantly, of the choices made into the sample, pupils tended to choose friends who were similarly ranked within the setting system. Interviews with pupils suggest that this was not a random, unconscious outcome of pupils bumping into each other in classes (which were in any case derived from the streaming system). Consider the comments of Morris and David.

Table 10: *Distribution of friendship choices across S[2] scores*

No. of pupils	Choices From	Choices To			
		S[2] = 2–4	S[2] = 5–7	S[2] = 8–10	Totals
55	S[2] = 2–4	162(2.95)	51(1.13)	12(0.44)	225
45	S[2] = 5–7	49(0.89)	111(2.47)	34(1.26)	194
27	S[2] = 8–10	12(0.22)	25(0.56)	58(2.15)	95
127	Totals	223	187	104	514

Notes:
1 $X^2 = 219$ df = 4 p <.005
2 188 (26.8 per cent) of the grand total of 702 choices were outside the sample.
Numbers of friendship choices received per pupil in that S[2] range score are bracketed.

Morris $S[2] = 2$.
Well there are some kids that I don't like but I wouldn't say there is any *one* I particularly dislike. The best way to define them is pupils in the lower sets and in the second year they were sort of enemies but now I'm in different classes to them and don't mix with them any more except in registration.

David $S[2] = 10$. [Previously David had stated that he disliked 'boffins']
— Who are these people who have become boffins and what are they?
— Well, last year I used to have a friend Charley [Charley was in the top sets for English, mathematics and French] but this year he doesn't speak to me any more and every time I see him he's hanging around with boffins like. When I go round to his house, now and again, he's always got his 'O' level and 'A' level books open and he's always concentrating on his work. Hanging around with boffins.
— What are boffins?
— People who work. Stay in all the time. Never go out, go down the town or nothin. And always get good letters home and pats on the back by teachers.

Similarly, Charley told me that he thought his friendships had changed over the years due to being in different sets and due to 'intellectual differences'.
    In addition, in an informal interview situation twenty-six pupils were asked about their reasons for liking–disliking teachers. Responses indicated a strong association between streaming and the common concerns of pupils. Typically, pupils with a low S[2] (especially $S[2] < 5$) stated that they liked teachers with whom they had 'made a lot of progress', who 'you could have a joke with but then get down to work'. The majority of these pupils mentioned that they disliked teachers who 'let other people

mess about all the time', 'who can't control the class'. By contrast, the pupils with high S[2] (especially S[2] > 7) typically liked teachers 'who aren't bossy', 'you can have a laugh because he can't control the class so you can take advantage'. The majority of the lower streamed pupils mentioned disliking teachers because they 'have a go at you for the slightest thing and send you down to the work centre', 'really strict', 'who've got pets', 'separate me from the rest of the class 'cause I'm always talking and then sending me down to the work centre'.

Essentially the pupils streamed in the top sets tended to be concerned about making academic progress and desired 'strict' teachers to help them achieve academically. This common concern is not merely a function of being in many of the same classes; it is a pro-school value-system which is associated with the position of these classes in the streaming hierarchy. Similarly, the common concern of the bottom-set pupils with being reprimanded and wanting to 'have a laugh' reflects their anti-school value-system rather than merely the fact that they tend to be in the same classes.[6] These kinds of values, then, are more persistent and deeply felt than the 'interaction sets' discussed by Furlong (1976).

Sociometric analysis of the eight classes revealed that the top sets E1, M1 and F1 were all dominated by friendship groups with pro-school value systems, though E1 and M1 each had an isolated anti-school friendship group. By contrast, the bottom sets E5 and M5 were dominated by anti-school friendship groups though each had a pro-school friendship group and some pro-school isolates. Unlike Ball (1981), I found the pupils streamed in the middle to be more pro-school in their value orientations than the pupils streamed at the bottom. For example, E3 was dominated by pro-school values and M3 and F2 tended to accommodate a mixture of commitments to the school values.

The complex friendship patterns of the middle sets are best understood by considering one in further depth (Figure 1). For the sake of brevity I shall not discuss in detail the entire sociomatrix, but only a representative subsample of it.

1 **George** no CAT st, n[b.b.] = 6, n[m.a.] = 7, S[2] = 5.
   This pupil had clearly defined anti-school values. He told me that most teachers disliked him and that he did not like them. According to the school records he had got 'into trouble' for 'vandalizing an electric socket'. On the descending scale of 1–5 for 'behaviour' the teacher of M3 gave him a grade 3. George estimated that he had been sent down to the 'work centre' five times that year and was in no doubt that leaving school would mean 'freedom' for him. He was an isolate in M3 but he was linked to an anti-school group in F2 through his friendship with Alan in F2. Alan fell into the 'bad–bad' category mentioned earlier. George estimated that he

Figure 1: *Socio matrix of M3*

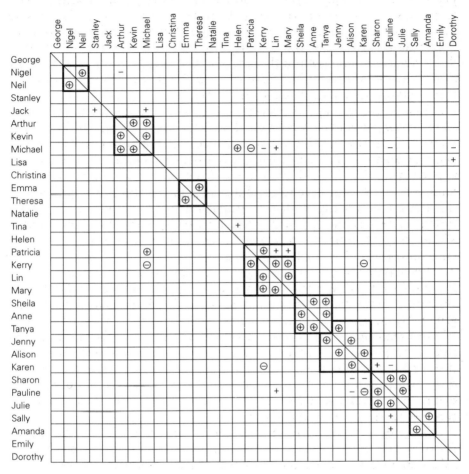

⊕ = RECIPROCATED FRIENDSHIP CHOICE
+ = UNRECIPROCATED FRIENDSHIP CHOICE
⊖ = RECIPROCATED DISLIKE
− = UNRECIPROCATED DISLIKE

spent less than 1 hour per week on his English and mathematics homeworks combined.

Stanley and Jack were also anti-school pupils who were isolates in M3.

2 **Natalie** CAT st = 8.33, n[b.b.] = 0, n[m.a.] = 0, S[2] = 6.
Natalie clearly held pro-school values. She wanted to study further at school and had received many notes for 'good behaviour'. She also received a 1 for 'behaviour' from the teacher of M3. She

was an isolate in M3 and E3 despite the fact that the dominant value-system of E3 was pro-school. She spent at least four hours on her combined English and mathematics homework per week.

Lisa, Christina and Tina were also pro-school pupils who were isolates in M3.

3 **Pair: Nigel and Neil** Averages: CAT st = 6, n[b.b.] = 5, n[m.a.] = 0.5, S[2] = 6.5.

These pro-school pupils were rarely rebuked in class and both had received a considerable number of notes for 'good behaviour'. Both received a grade 2 for 'behaviour' from the teacher and spent two hours or more weekly on their combined English and mathematics homeworks. Neil was also part of a pro-school friendship group in E3.

The only other friendship group which was clearly pro-school was that between Sharon, Pauline and Julie.

4 **Group: Kerry, Lin and Mary** Averages: CAT st = 6.8, n[b.b.] = 27.7, n[m.a.] = 3, S[2] = 5.33.

Patricia was linked to this friendship group by her friendship with Kerry. The tightly knit threesome of Kerry, Lin and Mary formed a strongly anti-school group. Kerry spent less than two hours on her combined English and mathematics homeworks per week. Kerry said that she hated school and just wanted to 'get out'. She received a 5 for 'behaviour' in M3 and was consistently involved in arguments with the teacher. Lin and Mary also sat with each other in their English class, forming an isolated anti-school pair in the predominantly pro-school E1. They received grades 4 and 3 for 'behaviour' in M3 respectively.

There was no other clearly anti-school group in M3.

5 **Group: Sheila, Anne and Tanya** Averages: CAT st = 6.9, n[b.b.] = 3.7, n[m.a.] = 2.7, S[2] = 6.7. This group accommodated a variety of values from Sheila who was fairly anti-school to Tanya who was fairly pro-school to Anne who was clearly pro-school. Whilst Sheila received a grade 3 for 'behaviour' in M3, the others received a grade 2. Anne's commitment to the school values is indicated by her desire to do well at school so that she can 'plan a career'. This value position is reflected by the fact that she spent seven and a half hours per week on her combined English and mathematics homeworks.

There were other fairly pro-school groups like this one: Jenny, Alison and Karen; and Arthur, Kevin and Michael. Also the friendship pairs Emma and Theresa, and Sally and Amanda, can be described as fairly anti-school.

In addition, Helen's value orientation towards the school seemed extremely ambiguous. In the cases of Emily and Dorothy, who were both isolates in M3, little can be said about their value orientations because they did not complete the questionnaires or attend any of the other classes I observed.

This study of M3 illustrates several points related to differentiation. First, friendship choices outside the class were almost always to pupils of similar value orientations. Due to the polarization of predominant values between top and bottom sets, which I have already discussed, the committed pro-school pupils in the middle sets tended to choose their friends from the higher sets and committed anti-school pupils tended to choose theirs from the lower sets. Consequently, each value orientation is reinforced and polarization accentuated. However, for pupils such as Helen who was straddling the pro- and anti-school value systems no such reinforcement is guaranteed.

Secondly, although there are exceptions, such as Emma and Theresa, commitment to school values by the friendship group/pair or the individual tends to be positively related to commitment to homework/schoolwork. This indicates how *intra*-set polarization leads to differences in academic performance — the part of a cycle which provides the basis for further differentiation which my earlier data suggest leads to polarization.

Thirdly, polarization in M3 was not as acute as was found by previous research concerned with classes streamed by forms or bands. For example, there were many more isolates in M3 than in Ball's 2TA, Hargreaves' 4C or Lacey's 3E. Pupils such as George, Stanley and Jack, despite all being anti-school boys, did not come together in M3 to form a friendship group. Instead they were friendly with pupils in other classes and were prepared to endure the four hours per week in M3 as isolates. Hence the data suggest that setting creates a more dispersed form of polarization, than streaming by forms or bands.

And fourthly, it will be noted that all the friendship groups in M3 were single-sex. This was not true of all the other sets some of which included one or two mixed-sex friendship groups. However, the vast majority were single-sex across all sets in the sample. This is not, of course explained by setting. Certainly sex differences were found in pupils' values and perspectives on friendships. Like Lambart, I found that the girls tended to refer to very pro-school pupils as 'pets' rather than 'boffins' (a term commonly used by the boys). But, unlike McRobbie (1978), I did not find that the anti-school girls resented the 'pets' or the 'swots' because they did not like boys. Girls and boys gave many reasons for preferring to 'go about with' members of their own sex. For example, girls mentioned that boys sometimes harrassed them and that boys were 'show offs' and 'mouthy'. Sex and gender differences cannot, therefore, be ignored if one is to fully explain the friendship patterns shown in Figure 1. However, the evidence suggests that subcultural polarization into pro- and anti-school groups is certainly one important factor, and that this type of polarization of friendship patterns is associated with the ranking system of organizational differentiation.

This finding is supported by the fact that the friendship patterns in M3 and other sets divide along pro- and anti-school axes for *both* girls and boys even if the *nature* of pro- and anti-school values is sometimes different for boys and girls and different gender groups. This is not to suggest that the pro-/anti-school axis is some kind of 'base' and gender is an epiphenomenon. Rather it is to acknowledge that the two social forces have a degree of autonomy in affecting pupils' friendships and social interactions. In the next chapter I focus more fundamentally on the gender characteristics of friendship groups.

Conclusion

The evidence adduced in this chapter suggests that there are good reasons for supposing that organizational differentiation contributes to subcultural polarization in the setted comprehensive as well as in secondary schools practising the more rigid and dated types of streaming. My findings do not support Quine's research conclusions that there is no systematic relationship between pupils' ranking within the school system and their commitment to the school's behavioural norms. On the contrary, my study shows that there is a positive relationship between these two variables. This is important because streaming by sets, instead of by forms or bands, has been widely employed by headteachers to reduce or eliminate some of the effects of subcultural polarization that have been perceived by teaching staff. My research suggests that, at least in a fairly pressured academic environment, setting is unlikely to eliminate polarization effects and probably only reduces them marginally.

Since working-class pupils tend to be placed in the lower sets and middle-class pupils in the top sets, it follows that streaming also becomes a form of social-class differentiation in symbiosis with the dominant subcultural values of the sets. Thus, streaming by sets is likely to accentuate social-class differences in academic performance at school. Evidently streaming by sets is inconsistent with the egalitarian and integrative comprehensive ideals of bringing pupils together from different social-class backgrounds with a view to reducing social-class inequalities and increasing social solidarity.

Notes

1   I also constructed the indicator S[3] which represents a pupil's set-score on English 'plus' mathematics 'plus' French. As the association between French sets and S[2] suggests, S[3] and S[2] are also strongly correlated. However, the disadvantage of using S[3] as an indicator of the pupils' rankings is that it only applies to those pupils who opted for French.

2 Note that the totals columns for table 5 do not necessarily equal the sum of the individual annual frequencies because some of the missed assignment reports included in the totals calculations were undated and therefore could not be included in the annual figures. Of the 224 missed assignment reports considered, 20 (8.1 per cent) were undated. Similar remarks apply to b.b.s in table 6.

3 For pupils in the middle sets, third-year examinations were particularly significant because they would partly determine whether teachers considered a pupil to be appropriate for 'O' level studies versus CSE. Many middle-set pupils wanted to take the more prestigious 'O' level and it is likely that this was reflected in an accentuation of pro-school values (in terms of behaviour and schoolwork) within the middle sets in the third year.

4 These data do not take account of set changes over time. However, these are not significant. Discussions with teachers indicated that set changes in English and mathematics were infrequent and I detected very few in my study of pupil records.

5 Ideally one would include the whole fourth form in one's analysis but because of the setting system this would have meant observing across some twenty classes. This was an unmanageable task — one which does not arise with streamed or banded forms. Hence a manageable, but imperfect, methodological compromise was made.

6 These finding are supported by Woods (1979).

Chapter 5

Gender, Differentiation and Deviance

Differentiation does not only occur through formal organizational arrangements such as setting. It also arises through less conscious means such as teachers' expectations of pupils. This kind of informal differentiation can be extremely important. In fact, it can form the basis for formal structures such as streaming because teachers' expectations may affect their evaluation of pupils' academic performance and behaviour. However, from a methodological point of view it is much more difficult to demonstrate the dynamics of informal differentiation. Nevertheless, researchers should not shy away from 'messy' research topics because they cannot generate correlations and statistical significance tests. Sometimes less precise methods are needed to reach plausible conclusions.

This chapter is concerned with how the eight teachers of the classes I observed differentiated between pupils in ways that are pertinent to gender. I discuss some of my classroom observations in the light of teachers' expectations of pupils and consider how the gender dimensions of some of the deviant friendship groups may be related to the teachers' sex-stereotyping of pupils.

Teachers, Sex-stereotyping and Classroom Interaction

The teachers varied in their teaching experience from Ms Frost (age 23, teacher of M3) who was completing her probationary year to Mr Bird (age 41, teacher of M1) who had been teaching for nineteen years. The other teachers were Mr Counter (age 25 and teacher of M5), Ms McGuinness (age 30 and teacher of E3), Mr Clay (age 29 and teacher of E1), Mr Steel (age 37 and teacher of E3), Mr Sexton (age 38 and teacher of F1) and Mr Pebble (age 27 and teacher of F2).

These eight teachers were asked to name and describe the most and least typical boys and girls in their classes. Although setting was in some cases an intervening factor, it was possible to construct a typology of the teachers' pupil sex-stereotyping. Two of the teachers, who had given most thought to sex roles were challenging about the question initially. For example, Ms McGuinness said:

It depends what you mean by typically boyish . . . Interested in only things boys are interested in? Do you mean girlish as particularly feminine?

Nevertheless, I resisted demands to impose definitions on the teachers and allowed them to interpret the question in their own way. The reason for this is that I wanted the teachers to construct their own definitions. In terms of pupils mentioned by teachers with particular qualities there was a very large degree of overlap. Mr Bird was the only teacher not to give categorizations. He felt unable to do so and said it was because there were 'no real characters in M1'. All he would say was:

A girl tends to be neater than a boy — that's not girlish or boyish — it's a fact of life.

One might be justified in linking this statement to the operational category, say, 'typical girls are conscientious about their presentation of work', but since this was an isolated comment made without M1 particularly in mind I decided to exclude Mr Bird from this particular analysis, due to his failure to cooperate.

The comments of the other seven teachers could be divided into five basic categories. The first four categories are unambiguous, namely, 'least typical boys', 'most typical boys', 'least typical girls', and 'most typical girls'. Some teachers also referred to girls who were 'least typical' in some ways and 'most typical' in others. Hence the fifth category 'least and most typical girls'. The following list shows how the seven teachers described and defined girls and boys.

1	**Least typical boys**	These were described as effeminate, softly spoken like a girl, immature, lacks strength of personality, wants to sit with the girls, don't adopt their own stance, a bit creepy, conscientious, relates better to girls, enjoys gossiping and bitching.
2	**Most typical boys**	These were described as the cowboy faction, the lads, not bright academically, bored with school, don't want to work, get up to mischievous tricks, see a male teacher as someone they can have a laugh with, try to get by doing as little as possible, unwilling to let sensitivity show, always got to be seen and noticed in everything they do, flirt with girls, misbehave deliberately, have an active interest in the opposite sex.
3	**Most typical girls**	These were described as lacking in confidence, neat, fussy about their work and totally co-operative, conscientious, more ready to accept the

teacher's wishes, very bright and very pleasant but doesn't say much and very studious, very silly and gigglish, quiet and timid, work the hardest.

4 **Least and most typical girls**   These were described as aggressive, bothered by what others see in their appearance, discuss hair styles, boyfriends, etc., sexually mature, attractive, very concerned about their appearance.

5 **Least typical girls**   These were described as good organizers, scruffy and not at all feminine, bolshy, hang around with boys, don't have girls as friends, initiators, inclined to make up their own minds about things.

These comments reflect, to some extent, the teachers' expectations of the pupils according to their sex. What one considers typically girlish is directly related to one's expectations of girls. If these expectations are not fulfilled by a girl then she is considered untypical or less typical, and similarly for boys. There is nothing sinister about this. It is unsurprising as we live in a gendered and sexist society. On the other hand, if schools are to function as anti-sexist institutions then they must first confront the character and implications of their own sex-stereotyping.

Two important factors are immediately apparent from the teachers' comments. First, typical boys are considered more likely to raise 'behaviour problems' for teachers. This is also true of the less typical girls. From the point of view of classroom management, teachers expect boys to make more behaviour-corrective demands on them. Secondly, typical girls are considered to be conscientious but 'lacking in confidence', 'pleasant', 'timid', or possibly 'silly'. The evidence also suggests that teachers expect girls to be less verbal and outspoken. This is supported by the fact that being outspoken and taking initiatives is considered a quality of the least typical girls.

Tables 11 and 12 show that for nearly every S[2] score girls receive less m.a.s and b.b.s per pupil than boys. These reports are made by all the teachers, not just the eight accounted for by the typological data above. Tables 11 and 12 are consistent with the teachers' expectations of boys and girls. The fact that the boys receive more b.b.s and the girls receive less m.a.s could be seen as verification of the teachers' expectations that boys tend to generate more behavioural problems and girls tend to be more conscientious.

On the other hand, very few qualitative sex differences in the m.a.s and the b.b.s were found. Although more boys were reported for 'fighting' and more often, girls were also reported for this type of deviance. The only sex-specific types of deviant behaviour which were found from the reports were 'wearing jewellery' and 'showing her bottom' for girls and 'bringing in dirty magazines' for boys. Furthermore, the number of hours spent on English and mathematics homeworks do not strongly

Table 11:   Number of missed assignment reports (m.a.s) received

	Boys			Girls		
S[2]	n'	n[m.a.]	per boy	n	n[m.a.]	per girl
2	18	9	0.5	14	1	0.1
3	7	19	2.7	5	2	0.4
4	1	13	13.0	7	6	0.9
5	3	26	8.7	9	14	1.6
6	3	3	1.0	8	11	1.4
7	3	3	1.0	14	22	1.6
8	2	21	10.5	5	5	1.0
9	4	26	6.5	3	11	3.7
10	8	29	3.6	5	10	2.0
Totals	49	149	2.96	70	82	1.2

Table 12:   Number of 'bad behaviour' notes (b.b.s) received

	Boys			Girls		
S[2]	n	n[b.b.]	per boy	n	n[b.b.]	per girl
2	18	51	2.8	14	12	0.9
3	7	44	6.3	5	5	1.0
4	1	11	11.0	7	13	1.9
5	3	39	13.0	9	35	4.0
6	3	5	1.4	8	19	2.4
7	3	9	3.0	14	73	5.2
8	2	50	25.0	5	89	18.0
9	4	118	29.5	3	88	29.3
10	8	81	10.1	5	42	8.4
Totals	49	408	8.4	70	376	5.0

support the view that girls are much more conscientious. Tables 13a, b, c and d indicate that girls are not more conscientious than boys at mathematics and only slightly more conscientious at English.

Nevertheless, quantitative analysis of classroom interaction suggests that boys got rebuked significantly more than girls in most classes (Table 14). It is very difficult to demonstrate conclusively that this is the result of teacher expectations or whether it is merely what is reflected in their expectations. Observation, however, did reveal that the 'typical' anti-school boys tended to plan collectively ways of irritating the teacher in class in order to gain a response which would be a source of humour and this was identified by the teachers. None of the teachers had any difficulty identifying 'the lads'.

Anti-school girls, on the other hand, tended to object to the school's strictness in terms of classroom rules and other behavioural requirements. They usually showed their objections by pushing the rules to the limit and then acting as if the teacher's rebuke was a ridiculous imposition on their normal activity. A particularly common tactic was to pretend that the

Table 13a: Hours spent per week on English homework by boys

S[2]	n	< 1/2 hour	1/2–1 hour	1–2 hours	2–3 hours	3–4 hours	> 4 hours
2	18	0	1	8	9	0	0
3	7	0	2	3	2	0	0
4	1	0	1	0	0	0	0
5	3	0	1	0	1	1	0
6	3	0	1	2	0	0	0
7	3	0	0	3	0	0	0
8	2	1	0	0	1	0	0
9	4	1	0	2	1	0	0
10	8	1	3	2	2	0	0
Total	49	3	9	20	16	1	0

Table 13b: Hours spent per week on English homework by girls

S[2]	n	< 1/2 hour	1/2–1 hour	1–2 hours	2–3 hours	3–4 hours	> 4 hours
2	14	0	0	3	10	1	0
3	5	0	0	1	4	0	0
4	7	0	1	4	2	0	0
5	9	0	0	4	5	0	0
6	8	0	1	7	0	0	0
7	14	0	0	4	5	4	1
8	5	0	1	2	1	1	0
9	3	0	1	2	0	0	0
10	5	0	1	2	1	1	0
Total	70	0	5	29	28	7	1

Table 13c: Hours spent per week on mathematics homework by boys

S[2]	n	< 1/2 hour	1/2–1 hour	1–2 hours	2–3 hours	3–4 hours	> 4 hours
2	18	1	0	6	9	2	0
3	7	0	0	5	1	1	0
4	1	0	0	1	0	0	0
5	3	2	0	0	1	0	0
6	3	0	1	2	0	0	0
7	3	0	0	1	2	0	0
8	2	1	0	0	0	1	0
9	4	3	0	1	0	0	0
10	8	0	4	3	1	0	0
Total	49	7	5	19	14	4	0

Table 13d: Hours spent per week on mathematics homework by girls

S[2]	n	< 1/2 hour	1/2–1 hour	1–2 hours	2–3 hours	3–4 hours	> 4 hours
2	14	0	0	2	10	2	0
3	5	0	0	2	3	0	0
4	7	1	1	2	3	0	0
5	9	0	1	3	3	2	0
6	8	1	1	1	5	0	0
7	14	2	1	1	6	3	1
8	5	0	2	1	0	1	1
9	3	0	2	1	0	0	0
10	5	0	1	2	1	1	0
Total	70	4	9	15	31	9	2

Table 14: *Number of interactions per boy and per girl per lesson (first 25 minutes approximately)*

	Boys					Girls				
	T–P		P–T			T–P		P–T		
	Q	R	Q	A	r	Q	R	Q	A	r
M1	0.25	0.14	0	0	0	0.09	0	0.06	0	0.67
M3	0.04	0.71	0	0.04	0	0.05	0.15	0.08	0.01	1.6
M5	0.07	0.52	0.33	0.04	4.71	0.04	0.24	0.49	0	12.25
E1	0.35	0	0.04	0.31	0.12	0.08	0	0.08	0.18	1.0
E3	0.33	0.17	0.06	0.3	0.18	0.01	0.11	0.11	0.03	11.0
E5	0.2	0.4	0.04	0.03	0.2	0.13	0.1	0.13	0	1.0
F1	0.7	0.12	0.08	0.08	0.11	0.67	0.07	0.07	0.1	1.0
F2	0.75	0.17	0.28	0.17	0.37	0.64	0.18	0.57	0.27	0.89

Notes:
T–P = teacher to pupil; P–T = pupil to teacher; R = rebuke;
Q = verbal question; A = verbal answer;
r = ratio of questions posed by pupils to questions posed to pupils.

teacher's rebuke was preventing progress with school work implying that the teacher's discipline was wasting valuable time. Ironically, this was a tactic used on occasions to embarrass or isolate troublesome pupils in the top sets. Importantly, the girls' type of objection to school rules was practised in a more individual way and may not be seen as such a threat to classroom order. This probably goes some way to explaining the sex differences in the teachers' expectations of pupils, but the response that teachers gave to 'the lads' also partly explains their desire to continue with their deviance.

Table 14 reveals other sex differences in classroom interaction though some may be more related to pupils' perceptions of subjects than to teacher sex-stereotyping. On average, boys were asked many more questions in mathematics classes and some English classes but not in French. In French there seemed to be little difference in this regard. On the other hand, girls asked more questions than boys, on average, except in F1 where there was little or no sex difference. This evidence does not support the view that girls are typically timid or quiet with respect to the academic aspects of general classroom interaction. Further, girls gave more verbal responses to questions in French than boys but the opposite was true for mathematics. This suggests that in a context where girls can expect some success they are not timid but in a context where they are in the minority and feel that being a girl makes the work inappropriate they are less likely to offer responses than boys (some girls told teachers explicitly that mathematics is a boys' subject).

The ratio of questions posed *by* pupils to questions posed *to* pupils by the teacher was almost always much greater for girls than it was for boys. For example, in F1 it was 0.11 for boys and 1.0. for girls. In F2 it was 0.37 for boys and 0.89 for girls. In other words, on average, interactions which were questions about work were more frequently initiated by the teacher if his or her interaction was with a boy than vice versa. By contrast, if this type of interaction was between the teacher and a girl it tended to be initiated by the girl. We can draw two quite different conclusions from this evidence. On the one hand, it could be argued that because boys were asked more questions, girls felt more strongly than boys that they had to initiate interactions with the teacher in order to get attention — that is, the girls were acting to compensate for unconscious discrimination on the part of the teacher. On the other hand, we might suppose that the girls in this sample happened to be rather more questioning than the boys, and that the teacher was compensating for the quietness of the boys by asking them more questions. However, the latter supposition seems implausible because it is not consistent with the teachers' descriptions of typical girls and typical boys. Boys were not typically considered to be timid by the teachers. Hence, it is reasonable to conclude that these differences are more likely to have resulted from unconscious teacher discrimination.

Evidence from informal working situations indicates that the most typical boys gained a significant amount of attention, often through activities defined by the teacher as misbehaviour. My classroom observation suggests that where groups were allowed to form within the classroom, the 'most typical boys' group managed to secure most of the attention of the teacher. The following three examples illustrate how this came about.

Example 1   **Mr Steel: E5 lesson notes**
The pupils are asked to organize themselves into groups. The two main groups are a large boys' group and a large mixed group. There is also a small girls' group. I sat with the mixed group. The pupils are to use a tape recorder to record their opinions on a certain topic. The boys in the mixed group take total control of the tape recorder while the girls sit at the side and watch. On playing back his recording one boy makes fun of the other one by saying 'he sounds like a girl, sir'. Mr Steel helps the boys in the mixed group in between trying to get the all boys' group to work on their topics. He also attends to the girls' group but the centres of attention are certainly the all boys' group and the mixed group which is dominated by the activities of the boys. In fact, the girls in the mixed group did not get a chance to do any recording that lesson.

Example 2   **Mr Counter: M5 lesson notes**
The class is seated in about five groups. The teacher explains how results of a table are to be obtained. The teacher looks at what results some pupils have got and then goes around the classroom. One group of boys

chat a lot during the lesson. They are very noisy. The teacher threatens to split them up by making them sit with the girls. Most of the girls are quiet and working. There are four such groups. There is also a mixed group which is quite noisy. The girls in the mixed-group fool around with the boys. The most boisterous is the all boys' group. They seek a lot of attention from the teacher by fooling about and the teacher spends periods of up to five minutes, on and off, trying to get them to do some work whilst girls' hands are up asking for assistance on the other side of the room. Even when the teacher does go over to help some of the girls he has to shout across intermittently to the all boys' group to be quiet because he can't hear what the girl is asking him about.

Example 3   Ms Frost: M3 lesson notes

Teacher explains that formulae of the areas of various shapes are required for the exam. There is considerable talking. A group of boys is particularly noisy and the teacher instructs Nigel to sit away from his friends. He refuses and the battle of wills goes on for about five minutes before the teacher finally gives up. Meanwhile some girls at the back are calling the teacher for help and complaining about not getting it.

These were not isolated incidents. Nor did they represent deliberate policies on the part of the teachers to give more attention to boys. Instead they reflected a concern on the part of the teachers that the pupils should follow the academic norms of the school combined with their belief (held with some empirical validity) that the most typical boys were likely to present the most opposition to their aims in the classroom. The result was a polarization of involvement between the sexes. It was expected that boys would dominate and be attention seekers, but that girls would be quiet and conscientious. The teachers tended to work with these as 'givens' rather than to challenge them because that seemed to be the most viable management strategy in coping with the immediacy of many classroom situations. Nevertheless, this evidence confirms the findings in many other sociological studies of sex differences in education that girls' academic experience may be hampered by the way schools handle the behavioural conduct of boys (Delamont, 1990; Less, 1993; Riddell, 1992; Spender and Sarah, 1988).

The greater attention given to the boys by teachers did not go unfelt by the girls. A recurring theme in interviews with the girls was that boys were generally overrated by the school system. The following example is a good illustration of this:

Alison	All the teachers I didn't like, they always favoured the boys and never taught us — the girls.
JA	How did they favour the boys in their teaching?
Alison	It was usually the boys who were noisy in the class and if a girl put her hand up they always keep her waiting and just never get round to it. And if a boy and a girl put up their hand at the same time they'd always talk to the boy. They'd never have time for the girls.

This feeling was particularly marked in the case of PE. Twenty-three girls in the sample complained that boys got much more attention than girls in PE.

Pamela	Well, PE, which is not really a subject, we've got a male teacher who's really sexist. He thinks boys are great and he's really degrading to girls. He's always picking boys like his favourites to do things for him. He's really sexist, it's not right.
JA	How is he degrading to girls?
Pamela	He thinks they're a lot lower than him and he just shoves them out of the way. But a woman PE teacher says the girls are better and they have a little argument about it which I think is pathetic cause they're all equal I think.
Julie	In football, basketball and things the teacher goes 'Come on boys' and doesn't include the girls in any of the activities. We could do football and rugby an' that as well. There's only netball and badminton for the girls. The teacher thinks we're too sissy for football. The fact that I say they become sexist is because if you try to do football or learn to do something new they [the boys] take the mickey and laugh at us which is why the girls don't want to take part.

It is worth noting that these types of complaints did not come exclusively from anti-school girls. In fact, Alison, Pamela and Julie were all pro-school pupils who were rarely 'in trouble' and accepted the broad academic norms of the school. This implies that the girls' dissatisfaction cannot be attributed to blanket hostility towards the school and teachers. The sexual division of games in PE spilled over into lunch and breaktime in the most dramatic way. I was struck by the contrasting ways in which the fourth-year boys and girls would spend their breaks and lunchtimes. On the whole the boys would engage in some sort of pseudo football or cricket taking up large spaces, whilst the girls would sit on the grass and talk or walk around the school grounds chatting. Many other aspects of socially learned norms account for these sex-based divisions in lunchtime activities but clearly PE lessons served to reinforce them. This is another example of how the school situation can reinforce wider gender divisions.

Sex Differences and Gender Differences

As I discussed in Chapter 2 there have been numerous studies of boys' subcultures in schools. Most of these have focused on how boys develop 'anti-school' or 'counter-school' subcultures (Hargreaves, 1967; Lacey, 1970; Willis, 1977). In the 1970s other researchers (mostly women) pointed quite correctly to the absence of studies of girls' subcultures or groups in schools. The male dominance of sociology of education and the tendency of male researchers to consider boys as more exciting research subjects have been suggested as possible reasons (Acker, 1981; McRobbie, 1978). Whatever the reasons, several studies concentrating on girls' subcultures and groups became available.

These have shown, among other things, that generalizing from boys to all pupils is often not justified (Anyon, 1983; McRobbie, 1978). Research studies of girls have done much to develop the discussion of sex differences within schooling as well as provide important insights into how girls do, or do not, form subcultures. Because of the way sex and gender are intertwined these studies have added to an understanding of what is meant by feminine and masculine adolescent genders. However, most of the research concerned with school subcultures, whether taking boys or girls or both as samples, have neglected any explicit study of gender differences within the *same* sex. Although there are often implicit explorations of gender differences within a sample of boys or girls, usually differences between boys or between girls are related to some intervening variable such as social class, ability grouping or ethnicity.

Gender differences within the same sex, then, have been neglected in the sociology of education. Often the terms 'sex difference' and 'gender difference' are used interchangeably and though it is true that some gender differences are also identifiable as sex differences this is not always so. As Wood (1984) notes, studies of adolescent sex and sexuality have been rare in the sociology of education even amongst feminist research. As one of the first ethnographies to include a discussion of masculinity and sexism within boys' anti-school culture, Willis's *Learning to Labour: How working class kids get working class jobs* was an extremely significant work. Yet it gives the impression that working class boys' counter-school culture is, on the whole, sexist and machismo, and that the alternative group must be conformist and inept in their relationships with girls.

Despite the many insights of Willis there is a danger that the *counter-*school element of 'the lads''s *gender* might be exaggerated on account of their overall (particularly social class-derived) culture clash with the school. The first section of this chapter documented sex differences in classroom interaction; the remainder explores some of the gender characteristics of anti-school girls and the gender culture of boys from two different groups of anti-school pupils. I focus on the gender differences between the two groups of boys and consider whether gender as a category has an anti-school function with respect to boys and girls in ways not captured by Willis's study of working-class boys.

Elements of a Culture: Gender Codes and Anti-school Girls

A close friendship group of four girls, Anne (S[2] = 10), Mary (S[2] = 9), Liz (S[2] = 9) and Jenny (S[2] = 7) held anti-school values. Anne, Liz and Jenny all stated that they looked forward to leaving school with varying degrees of antagonism towards the school. Liz was the most antagonistic. She told me that she looked forward to leaving school because she would then 'be free and not be treated like a prisoner'. She continued:

> I dislike school and I only come because I have to, it's just like a prison camp. I wouldn't mind if there was no school uniform, we could leave school at break and dinner, choose our own subjects and be treated civilized — like humans, not like animals.

Jenny and Anne were less antagonistic and looked forward to leaving school because they were bored with it. Mary did not find school quite so distasteful and in fact she did not look forward to leaving school because she was concerned that she might not get a job.

Classified according to father's occupation Anne and Mary were manual working-class whilst Liz and Jenny were non-manual non-professional middle-class. Liz and Jenny considered 'childcare' as their favourite subjects. It was also second and third favourite subject for Mary and Anne respectively. Jenny wanted to be a children's nurse and Mary a nurse. Anne and Liz said that they had no idea what they would like to do in the future. In general, all these girls had made traditionally feminine fourth year options. In all cases biology was the preferred and only 'pure' science chosen. In addition three of these girls chose 'typing' and two chose 'home economics'. Thus, in terms of career expectations and subject options it is fair to say that these girls had a traditionally feminine profile and followed a 'reproductive sex-role code'.

Yet teachers identified them as untypical of girls because of their anti-school behaviour. This indicates the tremendous power of the stereotype of girls as quiet and conscientious. The implication is that because these girls were anti-school, teachers viewed them as untypical of girls and, therefore, were blind to their traditional sex-role expectations. This situation does not provide a very promising basis from which teachers might challenge girls to reflect critically on their future careers.

Whatever the shades of antagonism towards the school, one thing all these girls had in common was a propensity to get 'into trouble' with teachers. Often one of these girls was to be found queuing outside the deputy head's office waiting to be scolded for some misdemeanour. Often the girl in trouble would be accompanied by one of the others as a form of support. In addition, over the four years each of these girls had accumulated at least 27 b.b.s with an average of 35.8, mostly received in the third and fourth year. Anne claimed that in her fourth year she had been sent to the 'work centre' about once a week.

Anne and Liz came together for English in E5 with Mr Steel. He described them as 'bolshy' and 'hostile to teachers' interjections'. Their behaviour in class indicated that they resented the teacher's authority over them. Although they rarely disobeyed instructions outright they made it clear to the teacher and the rest of the class that their obedience was reluctant. Mr Steel regularly rebuked Anne or Liz for being out of uniform. These girls were very concerned about their appearance and wanted the freedom to be able to dress and wear make-up as they wanted — a sort of 'libertarian feminine dress code'. Although the girls did not mention the gendering created by the uniform it is interesting that Mr Steel, who felt uniform was important, included 'girls wearing trousers' when giving a list of their deviant acts.

It was rare for these girls to arrive for their class eagerly awaiting their lesson. More often they would sit down and begin talking about a party just past, a club they might be attending, or possibly some exciting incident which had just occurred in the school. They would continue to do this as if the teacher was not in the room and sometimes ignore the teacher's classroom instructions to 'settle down'. Inevitably, they would then be singled out for a rebuke or possibly separated. As Anne explains the scenario can easily culminate in a sentence to the 'work centre':

Anne Well he doesn't like me sitting beside anyone 'cause I talk all the time. He makes me sit on my own so he moves me from where I start sitting. Then I say why and he says 'You don't ask questions' and then he sends me to the work centre.

A cursory glance at the 'bad-behaviour' reports and an occasional conversation with teachers over lunch about some anti-school pupils immediately revealed that such 'talking back' to teachers was defined as a deviant act. However, these girls did not share that judgment. Rather like the 'wenches' discussed by Davies (1984) they felt that they should respond to teachers in the way the teachers treated them. As Jenny put it: 'I don't like it when they shout at you a lot. If teachers shout at you you tend to shout back to them.' Whilst the boys tended to interpret teachers who shouted at them as 'hard' the girls interpreted them as disrespectful. Their way of treating pupils was seen as a way to treat 'animals' not people. What they thought of as bad treatment by teachers tended to be taken as a personal affront.

The teachers, by contrast, believed that the school rules were necessary to maintain social control. On my first day at the school it was explained to me that each year wore a different pullover as part of the uniform. One reason given for this was that if a pupil was trying to disappear through a hedge or something in an attempt to leave school at lunchtime then even if the exact identity of the pupil could not be discerned the pullover would provide some information. Also some parts of the school grounds were out of bounds for certain years and the pullovers were again mentioned as an aid in 'policing' this rule.

For these girls there was a great division between teacher and pupil priorities. It was a 'them' and 'us' situation, but ultimately the teachers had the greater power. The girls would truant, smoke, 'give back cheek', 'refuse to move when asked', 'fight in class', throw pens around the class, bang their pencils down on the desk when asked to watch the board, give teachers false messages and so on. They had the power to irritate and challenge the teacher's authority in all these ways but ultimately, as one girl put it, 'you get done'.

The 'libertarian feminine dress code' was valued by all these anti-school girls. However, there were some gender differences between them regarding more direct relations with boys. Interestingly, the libertarian spirit was tempered by concerns about girls' self-respect in this context. Jenny, for example, disliked girls who 'flirted with boys':

JA   Why do you dislike Catherine?
Jenny She has got a reputation with boys. She'll sit there in class with her skirt up and she'll be pouting her nice bright red lipstick and nail varnish in class. She'll go up to a boy and ask him 'Will you go out with me?' and if he says no she'll ask another one.
JA   What is it you don't like about that?
Jenny It's not right for a girl to go flaunting herself at boys like that. If there's a party or something all the rumours are about her. She did this and that with boys. It annoys me to see her waste herself like that. Some girls really hate her and call her names like 'slag' or 'whore'.

These comments are suggestive of an emerging subcultural value system about girl–boy relations and not merely a reverence for traditional feminine norms associated with a virtual inability to be assertive. The latter are well illustrated by Kate:

74

JA   Are you interested in boyfriends at the moment?
Kate   Yes, I know there's a boy who fancies me at the moment.
        It's quite funny, he's trying to get up the courage to ask
        me out and keeps failing.
JA   Would you take the initiative with anyone you fancied?
Kate   I think I'd drop hints but I wouldn't be able to ask them
        out.

Mary had few reservations about mixing with boys and frequently sat with some of 'the lads' in M5. Mr Counter remarked upon this activity but commented that he was not suggesting Mary was 'tarty'. Nevertheless the fact that the teacher felt the need to make this qualifying remark indicates the extent of the disapproval of girls' 'flirtatious' behaviour. In fact, Mary was the least concerned about her appearance of the four girls and managed to drift comfortably in and out of the boys' company. Liz and Anne were indifferent to moral judgments about girls' behaviour and simply felt that they should be able to do whatever they wanted in their relationships with boys. These two girls, in particular, felt that many of the boys in their classes were too 'immature' for them.

In fact this girls' group and the other girls whom I interviewed frequently listed boys among their dislikes. Some complained that boys were 'a pain' because they 'show off in class' and are 'mouthy'. The general consensus amongst the girls interviewed was that friendships with other girls were more important than boyfriends in relationships because friendships with girls were more secure. Some girls had also decided to prioritize their work over possible relationships with boys.

Elements of a Culture: Masculinity and 'the Lads'

I quickly became aware of a group of working-class boys who referred to themselves as 'the lads'. There were eight such boys who were friends or associate friends. Four of them, Nigel, David, Ronnie and Mike, however, formed a closely knit friendship group and only these four will feature here. They were all in the bottom sets (S[2] = 10). They all had manual working-class job aspirations such as 'car mechanic', 'builder' and 'carpenter'. Mike's father had a small menswear shop and his mother worked as a 'cleaning lady' in a canteen. He might be defined as having a lower middle-class or working-class background depending on one's classification. The others were of indisputably manual working-class backgrounds.

All these boys looked forward to leaving school because they thought it was a 'dump' and leaving would bring them 'freedom' — 'no nagging of teachers'. David and Ronnie did mention, however, that leaving school might be unfortunate because they would miss their 'mates'. This ambivalence derived from the fact that 'the lads' tended to use the school context as a *resource* for 'havin a laugh' or 'chatting up the teacher'. They would sit together in class and plan ways of fooling the teacher, call out joke answers to the teachers' questions and so on.

In conversation with me some of the teachers also referred to these boys as 'the lads' or 'the cowboy faction'. Although 'the lads' provided their own audience for each other they were always willing to extend their audience to a friendly observer and I found myself being regularly invited to sit with them. During their time at the school they had all been either suspended or sent to the 'work centre'. All had had letters sent home to their parents about unsatisfactory work or behaviour and all except Mike had been involved in fighting in the school. Each was keen to recount their confrontation with the school's rules especially if they had in some sense 'got away with it'. For example:

> **Mike** The other day me and some friends got done for shouting abuse — calling the caretaker names an' that and we got called for detention by Mr Fielding [the headteacher] and we didn't go. Fielding's always got something on his mind so he forgets! The day before we'd been havin' a laugh with the caretaker and then this time David decided he'd take advantage and start calling him names so we got done.

Mr Pebble was popular with David and Ronnie 'cause you can have a bit of a joke with him'. The feeling seemed to be reciprocated since Mr Pebble told me that he generally got on better with boys because they had more in common with him such as in sports — football etc. Ronnie and David were particularly interested in football and they would also play football regularly at lunchtime.

Part of the identity of these boys was defined by their sense of distinctiveness from girls. Inevitably this involved defining girls and girls' roles rather narrowly yet it was this sharp dichotomy between the sexes in their perceptions which led females to be regarded as objects of sexual fantasy and also of mystery.

The definition of masculinity outlined by 'the lads' lends some support to Willis's thesis that it is derived from the reproduction of shopfloor culture,' but the domestic division of labour was also important.

> **David** In CDT [Craft, Design and Technology] and PE boys get more attention 'cause they're doin' something like football or rugby but with childcare or typing or home economics girls get more attention 'cause it's their kind of subject.
>
> **JA** Why do you say it's their sort of subject?

> **David** Because women do the cooking, it's a girl's subject whereas with CDT you don't see women working in a factory with technology you see a man so it's a boy's subject or a man's subject.

Overall these boys viewed the girls as unexciting in class. For 'the lads' the girls do not, and cannot, contribute to 'havin' a laugh'.[2] Nevertheless, 'the lads' were acutely interested in girls and women from a heterosexual point of view. Importantly the attraction was almost exclusively built on images rather than relationships.

All 'the lads' claimed to have had girlfriends although Nigel admitted that his girlfriends usually only lasted for about a week. However, the distance that 'the lads' kept from any relationships with girls meant that there was a great deal of uncertainty involved in any interactions they did initiate. This is highlighted by the prospect of one of 'the lads' acting on his sexual desires.

> **JA** Do you have any girlfriends now?
> **Ronnie** No, like a load though.
> **JA** Are they at this school?
> **Ronnie** Yeah, some of them are.
> **JA** Have you done anything about it?
> **Ronnie** No, haven't got the courage. I'm too embarrassed but I might pluck up the courage one day.
> **JA** Are they fourth years?
> **Ronnie** I don't know them. I don't even know their names. I know one is a fourth year.

Not surprisingly Ronnie was rather nervous about 'asking out' a girl whose name he did not even know. This illustrates further the importance of 'looks' and images to 'the lads''s sexual preferences. It also indicates the price that the boys paid for their culture of masculinity. Accompanying the idea that 'a lad' needed to be able to boast about girlfriends was a high cost of rejection by a girl. Risking such rejection, therefore, required 'courage', and fantasy could be a more tolerable form of sexual being when 'courage' was not forthcoming. In addition, the heterosexual fantasy had a straightforward lineage with the use of the school situation as a resource for excitement. Just as teachers were there to tease so female bodies are visually available to be sexually objectified and during the boredom of the school day 'the lads' moved easily from one activity to the other.

Fighting was seen as an acceptable way of resolving certain disputes with other boys including disputes about girls.

> **JA** Do you get into any fights?
> **Ronnie** Had a fight with David in the second year. That was over one of my girlfriends.

JA What happened?

Ronnie Well, I was going with this girlfriend and he started calling her names and I didn't like it. He said he was only
taking the mickey and then we started squabbling in the
dinner queue and ended up punching. But David's one
of me best mates now.

The physicality of these boys as signalled by fighting was also a way
in which they could define power relations and status. Fights were always
recalled with tremendous detail and boys who were just 'all mouth' earned
no respect. One final characteristic of 'the lads''s masculinity was their
periodic shouting in a loud, rough voice, imitating an angry male teacher.
Using this voice they would shout at another pupil in the hope that the
reaction would be a source of amusement.

Elements of a Culture: Masculinity and the 'Gothic Punks'

One friendship group which had a high profile in the school was the
'gothic punks', as they described themselves. In my sample there were
five in all, namely, Alan, Malcolm, Tony, Kate and Susan. Tony and
Susan were of lower professional middle-class backgrounds (II) and Alan,
Malcolm and Kate were lower middle class (IIIN). None of the boys had
working-class manual job aspirations. Alan and Tony wanted to go to
some type of art-related technical college and Malcolm did not know nor
apparently care about a future job. Their friendships were not explained
by the streaming system. For the main academic subjects Alan (S[2] = 8)
was in the bottom ability stream, Malcolm (S[2] = 5) the middle, and Tony
(S[2] = 2) the top. These boys were identified by the teachers as untypical
of boys.

The 'gothic punks' were noticeable for two reasons. Firstly, they
were a fairly closely knit *mixed* sex group and, secondly, part of their style
was to wear all black clothing. The school uniform varied for different
years but for fourth years it was mostly grey and not black. Consequently,
the 'gothic punks' were regularly ticked off for being out of uniform and
in the case of Malcolm several letters from the headteacher and deputy
headteacher complaining about his 'appearance' were sent home to parents. Malcolm not only dressed in black, he also dyed his long hair and
wore conspicuous long pointed 'rocker' style boots. He was frequently in
trouble and sent to the 'work centre'. Like the anti-school girls at Greenfield
the 'gothic punks' held libertarian values about dress. Similarly, Alan and
Mark were sent to the 'work centre' for 'bad behaviour'. Alan was also
known to the school for truanting ('blunking off') but according to the
'gothic punks' themselves they all truanted. It was interesting that this fact

emerged rather casually in conversations rather than in the way 'the lads' would boast about their rule-breaking exploits. For example:

JA   Do you know where Susan is?
Alan   Yeah, she decided to have a day off. She's gone up to London.

Alan's response was given in a tone which would have been equally appropriate had he been telling me that Susan was in her French lesson.

Like 'the lads', the male 'gothic punks' all stated that they hated school. They claimed to spend less than half an hour per week on mathematics homeworks and an equally small amount of time on English homeworks except for Tony who would spend less than half an hour on mathematics and between two and three hours per week on English. Their school records implied that this was probably accurate since despite repeated ploys, such as pretending to have forgotten homeworks, they received many missed assignment reports. However, they can be contrasted with 'the lads' in several ways.

First, there was a rejection of the idea that scientific and technological subjects are the ones for boys. All these boys had art as their favourite subject and Alan had opted for home economics, his third favourite subject. Although he had chosen physics in preference to biology, this was not because he thought physics was a better subject for a boy, but because he objected to dissecting animals — an objection usually voiced by girls (Measor, 1983). Secondly, they rejected the mainstream masculine sports such as football and rugby. They suggested that these should be replaced by 'setting up bands within the school', 'running' and 'rock climbing — generally more exciting things'. As a mixed group the 'gothic punks' 'went round to each other's houses to listen to music and talk' or 'went to see bands'. This kind of leisure activity is reminiscent of the girls' groups of 'teeny boppers' reported by McRobbie (1978) rather than the all-male gangs similar to Willis's 'lads'. Malcolm claimed to be out every night and Alan helped to run a disco once a week. And thirdly, they complained about the machismo elements of their enemies. For example:

JA   What do you dislike about Philip?
Alan   Well, he's a casual but he's overviolent.[3] It's stupid really. Like in physics they're always sitting at the other table and they're insulting us. So I asked him what is it they've got against us and he told me to shut-up and asked me if I wanted a fight which isn't really a great response. Stupid.
JA   Have you been in any fights?
Alan   No, I try to avoid them.

A recurring theme for these boys was a rejection of 'the lads''s form of masculinity whether reflected by pupils or teachers:

Malcolm	I don't like people who think they're hard. In the corridor they might shout after me 'freak'. They'll say 'get your hair cut'. They just make comments about the way I dress 'cause it's not the same as them.
JA	Do teachers make comments about your dress or appearance?
Malcolm	Well Mr Fielding suspended me for it. That was when I wore what he described as a scruffy overcoat. When I wore a nice pair of big boots I got told not to wear them or my black jeans.
JA	What sort of things make you dislike teachers?
Alan	Depends on their whole attitude. Well Mr Shuttle and Mr Pebble are always ones to make out they're right lads. I just think they're prats.

Another striking difference between the male 'gothic punks' and 'the lads' was the absence of objectifying girls or women as sexual objects, at least in open conversation. They tended to speak about female 'gothic punks' as companions with whom they socialized and their 'girlfriends' were people they went out with a lot and had a good time.

The 'gothic punks' were unpopular with some of the teachers. Mr Pebble, who Alan had described as someone who tried to be 'one of the lads', told me at the end of a lesson in which he had sent Alan to the 'work centre':

I don't like that boy. There's a whole gang of them that are into drinking, drugs and God knows what.

He also described Alan as 'effeminate', 'softly spoken like a girl' and 'unusual for a boy of his age because he always sits with the girls'. This teacher engaged in activities which he himself described as 'laddish' such as going out on a Saturday night with 'the lads in the team after a football match'.

This teacher also admitted that he generally preferred teaching boys because he had more in common with them. He was fond of some of 'the lads' in the class even though they appeared to be no more committed to schoolwork than Alan. The implication is that it was essentially the differences in gender orientations that led to the conflict between Alan and Mr Pebble. The deputy headteacher also made similar comments and clearly identified with teaching groups of boys as 'lads'. It was equally clear that he disapproved of the lifestyle of the 'gothic punks'. On one occasion after disciplining Malcolm and Alan, the deputy headteacher remarked: 'Some of the fourth year in this school [referring to Malcolm and Alan and possibly other "gothic punks"] are trying to grow up too quickly.'

Frequently the 'gothic punks' gave the impression that they had outgrown school, and that it had become a tedious infringement on their 'real lives'. As Tony put it 'I hate school, it takes up so much of my time.' Rather like the 'wenches' studied by Davies (1984), the 'gothic punks' saw school as irrelevant to the most important aspects of their lives which concentrated on music, night life and relationships. Thus the gender profile of the male 'gothic punks' was not machismo and in some ways it had similarities with previous studies of some anti-school girls' groups and the anti-school girls at Greenfield. This indicates that not all anti-school boys fit the 'model' of Willis's 'lads'. It also suggests that gender divisions between pupils of the same sex is also an important factor in understanding pupil relations in school.

Polarization and Resistance

As the evidence in this chapter suggests, not all subcultural polarization amongst the pupil population can be attributed to organizational differentiation such as streaming. Gender codes and norms are also very important. As an institution the school tended to reinforce, rather than challenge traditional gender norms, albeit unconsciously. Girls who mixed too much with boys ran the risk of being labelled as 'slag' or 'whore' by pupils, and as untypical by teachers. Gender-based polarization occurred due to both sexual division, which results from only certain behaviours being seen as appropriate for each sex in the school environment, *and* gender division within the same sex which usually results from some members of that sex breaking certain norms of behaviour for that sex.

There was notable polarization between the two groups of boys discussed in this chapter which derived from the gender differences between them. Regarding the 'gothic punks', polarization from 'the lads' was implicit in their rejection of values and interests held by teachers or pupils who could be identified as defining themselves as 'lads'. 'The lads' themselves were much more explicit in their objection to the behaviour of 'effeminate' male 'gothic punks'.

JA   Why do you not like Alan? [David had put Alan as one of his dislikes on his friendship questionnaire]

David   He's always hanging on to girls and he's mouthy. He's all mouth. That's what most of them are like.

JA   What do you mean he's always hanging on to girls?

David   Well most of us go around with boys and girls but he just goes around with girls even in class. That's all he does, he even talks like a girl.

The phrase 'hanging on to' was one which was reserved for this kind of 'effeminate' behaviour. Normally 'the lads' would talk about 'hanging *around*' with boys. The 'hanging on to' metaphor implied an unmanly activity in which the boy was attaching himself to girls for security rather like hanging on to a parent's apron. It is also significant that David's dislike for Alan was justified by the 'normality' of allegedly what most of the boys did. Although the 'gothic punks' were unusual, David's view was inaccurate, at least for the fourth years in the school. The vast majority of friendship groups were single-sex (particularly including 'the lads') and the 'gothic punks' were a mixed-sex friendship group. In fact, if 'normality' were to be defined by 'going around with boys and girls' it would have been 'the lads' rather than the 'gothic punks' who were unusual.

The main objection 'the lads' had to the male 'gothic punks' was their breaking of gender codes, e.g., having girls as 'steady' friends as well as girlfriends. This polarization was reinforced in the school by teachers regularly threatening disruptive boys with the 'punishment' of being made to sit with the girls, and teachers who viewed the behaviour of 'the lads' with greater sympathy than that of 'gothic punks'.

Whether or not the behaviour of the male 'gothic punks' represented any resistance to the dominant gender relations in the school is a different matter. Aggleton and Whitty (1985) studied a group of middle-class anti-school boys and girls. Their research was mostly concerned with the degree to which those pupils could be seen as resistors to dominant social-class and gender relations. They found that only some of the girls offered criticisms of patriarchal relations and seemed to conclude that since they did not become 'actively oppositional' to patriarchal relations little 'resistance' was evident.

Certainly I found no evidence that the 'gothic punks' were 'actively oppositional to the continuance of patriarchal relations in general' (Aggleton and Whitty, 1985). Hence it may be more correct to define them as 'recusants' rather than resistors (Walker, 1985). The same was true of the anti-school girls' group. However, some of the pro-school girls, whom I interviewed, mentioned various injustices which they felt were sexist. Assertions that boys and girls should be treated equally were commonly made by these girls. A minority of the girls had no interest in the issue of sexual inequality and one girl told me she thought 'this whole business about sexism is a load of rubbish'. Nevertheless, when asked to give an opinion many girls took a stance that opposed certain elements of patriarchy. In E3 the girls were asked to write on whether they thought an advertisement for cars which used women as part of the attraction was sexist and if so why. Although most of the boys used some contorted reasoning to argue that the advertisement was not sexist most of the girls thought that it was, and some argued that this sort of advertising should be banned. This may not count as 'active opposition' but it does signal emerging criticism of patriarchal cultural values.

The 'gothic punks' reserved their criticism for the schooling system as a whole. For example, Malcolm scrawled on his questionnaire:

The system is f**ked. The teachers don't care if you don't try, they just give up on you and leave you to rot in the corner.

Later when I asked him why he thought this about 'the system' he replied: 'It doesn't really work unless you're good at academic subjects. They do well and everybody else doesn't.'

The 'lads', on the other hand, never talked about 'the system' and, although they disliked the 'boffins' and 'creeps', they believed that the 'boffins' and 'creeps' were 'brainy' or 'really bright'. I found little or no evidence to support the contention that 'the lads' were resisting the school as a system even though they experienced excitement in their tension with certain elements of the system.

The anti-school girls' group was quite different from 'the lads' in this respect. These girls directed most of their criticisms at the systemic aspects of the school to which they objected, such as school uniform, compulsory subjects and rules about pupil mobility. Regarding Walker's conditions of resistance of having a desire to see the system changed and replaced by another one, the 'gothic punks' and the anti-school girls seemed to be much more committed than 'the lads'.

Conclusion

Deviance is partly defined along gender axes. Consequently, it can act as a lever of gender differentiation and did so in Greenfield in terms of teachers' attention to boys and girls. Furthermore, the way in which teachers identified pupils as deviants seems to have been affected by their sex-stereotyping which, in turn, was related to their gender-value systems. This process of deviant labelling was most marked where there was a confrontation between the gender-value systems of the teacher and the pupil.

For example the teacher of F2, Mr Pebble, was particularly opposed to the breaking down of traditional sex roles. He felt he had a lot more in common with the typical boys and 'the lads'. Mr Pebble did not like Alan and remarked upon his effeminate manner in a rather disapproving tone. Reciprocally, Alan disliked Mr Pebble because he was 'always making out to be one of the lads'. It is fairly clear that a clash of gender-value systems was operating. Both disapproved of the other's behaviour and that disapproval was influenced by their respective gender-value systems. The power relationship, however, was not a reciprocal one and it was the pupil who became the institutional deviant not the teacher.

As regards gender, 'the lads' in my study (which have many similarities with Willis's 'lads') were less of a *counter*-school culture than the 'gothic punks'. Indeed, the practices of some of the teachers rested on the same fundamental assumptions about sex roles and gender as were held by 'the lads'. Institutionally, the school uniform also acted as a continual reminder of how a boy should look as compared with a girl. The 'gothic punks' (females and males) complained about the uniform, whereas 'the lads' generally accepted it.

Jackson and Marsden[4] (1962), Willis (1977) and others have been right to describe the social-class culture clash between working-class pupils and the middle-class school, but it may be an oversimplification to locate 'the lads''s version of masculinity as a subset of *counter*-school culture.[5] Even in the case of Willis's outspoken 'lads', it was rarely their sexism *per se* which involved them in conflict with the school, though their form of masculinity sometimes led to fighting and other types of behaviour defined as disruptive by the school authorities. Insofar as 'the lads''s sexism is part of their working-class culture one could argue that one reason why they tend to obtain masculine working-class jobs is because the school does not explicitly counter these boys' assumptions about gender.[6]

Notes

1 It is of course more correct to say a reproduction of shopfloor culture as perceived by 'the lads'. In fact, many women work with technology in factories. In his account Willis seems to accept the view of 'the lads' too uncritically, seemingly assuming that shopfloor culture is a male preserve.
2 These boys also felt that 'the boffins' had nothing to offer their exploits in class. 'The lads' defined these as pupils who worked a great deal at their academic work and did not go out in the evenings.
3 'Casuals' were people who dressed 'traditionally' and 'smartly'. The 'gothic punks' disliked 'casuals' of either sex.
4 Jackson and Marsden (1962) studied a sample of boys and girls.
5 Certain very visible aspects did bring conflict with the school. For example, pupils caught with pornographic magazines (what the school referred to as 'dirty magazines') were cautioned and sometimes a letter was sent home to parents reporting the incident. On the other hand, one teacher (male) told me that he had no objections to pupils looking at nude women in daily newspapers.
6 This is not to say that the school had any conscious policies of sexism. On the contrary, there was a conscious policy to encourage girls to opt for science subjects together with a common interest amongst many of the teachers in equality of opportunity between the sexes. However, the 'hidden curriculum' was a much more important factor in defining the school's impact upon the genders of 'the lads' and the 'gothic punks'.

Chapter 6

The Subject-option Process: Pupil Choice in School Knowledge

At Greenfield the transition from the third year to the fourth and fifth years involved the pupils in a process of opting to study some subjects further, and to discard others. Pupils could also take up new subjects. However, English, mathematics and one of the three main science subjects were compulsory. The complete list of option subjects was as follows: art, biology, CDT (craft, design and technology), chemistry, childcare, computer studies, drama, French, geography, German, history, home economics, humanities, music, PE, physics, RE, Spanish, technology, and typing. This is not to say that any combination of subjects could be opted for. Administrative expediency permitted only some combinations.

The school administration intervened in the option process, reducing the pupil's 'freedom of choice' in some cases. It should be noted that throughout this chapter the term 'opting' is not synonymous with 'choosing'. For the purposes of the following discussion an option is defined as the subject which a pupil finally follows at the school. This is not always the same as the pupil's original choice within the subject-option process.

Bearing in mind the correlation between streaming and social class (Tables 2a and 2b), we can see from Tables 15 and 16 that pupils in the lower streams (usually working-class) were more likely to opt for 'minority' subjects and 'practical' subjects than pupils in the top stream (usually middle-class) who tended to opt for mainstream higher status 'academic' subjects instead. Statistically these results are highly significant and they confirm the previous research by Ball (1981).

The usual sex differences were also found to apply to this sample as regards subject options. As Table 17 shows, 82 per cent (41 out of 50) of the boys followed two or more science options whilst this was the case for only 43.8 per cent (32 out of 73) of the girls. Similarly, 74 per cent (54 out of 73) of the girls followed two or more arts options but only 52 per cent (26 out of 50) of the boys did so. Such results are very consistent with the previous findings of Kelly (1981), Pratt *et al*. (1984) and Riddell (1992).

These overall trends are brought into sharp focus by considering some of the subjects for which gender and social-class polarization was greatest. For example, no boys opted for either childcare or typing and only seven girls from the top stream opted for either of these subjects whereas ten

Table 15: Distribution of options into 'academic' and 'practical' subjects across streams

		Practical			Academic			Totals		
Stream	n	N	%	Npp	N	%	Npp	N	%	Npp
Top	53	47	17.3	0.9	225	82.7	4.2	272	100	5.1
Middle	43	74	33.8	1.7	145	66.2	3.4	219	100	5.1
Bottom	27	62	48.1	2.3	67	51.9	2.5	129	100	4.8

Notes:
1 $X^2 = 43.56$ $p < 0.001$ $df = 2$
2 'Practical' subjects are art, craft design and technology (CDT), childcare, computer studies, home economics, technology, and typing. 'Academic' subjects are all other options (including the one compulsory 'pure' science).
3 n = number of pupils, N = number of options, % = percentage of practical or academic options in that stream, Npp = number of options per pupil in that stream.

Table 16: Distribution of options into 'main' and 'minority' subjects across streams

		Main			Minority			Totals		
Stream	n	N	%	Npp	N	%	Npp	N	%	Npp
Top	53	238	87.5	4.5	34	12.5	0.6	272	100	5.1
Middle	43	149	68.0	3.5	70	32.0	1.6	219	100	5.1
Bottom	27	78	60.5	2.9	51	39.5	1.9	129	100	4.8

Notes:
1 $X^2 = 42.87$ $p < 0.001$ $df = 2$
2 'Minority' subjects are the fourth-year options childcare, computer studies, humanities, technology, and typing plus options which were available for study in the third year which were CDT, German, home economics, and Spanish.
3 'Main' subjects are those which were part of the curriculum in the first, second and third years and continue to be in the fourth year. These are art, biology, chemistry, French, geography, history, music, and physics.

Table 17: Participation of boys and girls in arts and science subjects

No. of subject type taken	Boys		Girls	
	Science	Arts	Science	Arts
None	0	5	0	1
One	9	19	41	18
Two	18	17	29	29
Three	20	9	3	18
Four	3	0	0	7
Totals	50	50	73	73

girls from the lower streams opted for childcare and thirty-two girls from the lower streams opted for typing. Although as many as ten boys opted for home economics as compared with eighteen girls no pupils from the top stream opted for this subject. Similarly, only two of the fourteen boys opting to follow CDT were in the top stream. It is clear that few top-stream pupils opted for 'non-academic' lower-status subjects although one apparent exception to this trend was that nine top-stream boys opted for technology — 64 per cent of the total number of boys in the sample opting for that subject. Furthermore, very few girls opted for traditionally masculine subjects. For example only one girl opted for technology and only two for CDT. Within high-status 'academic' science the usual trend of biology being the only science into which more girls than boys opted was also found.

Previous research on the subject option process has tended to focus on either how one social group (e.g., working-class girls) perceive the process or on how a large sample of pupils relate to a particular subject/set of subjects (e.g., science). The approach here is rather different in that it is concerned with a small sample of boys and girls taken from the whole ability range as defined by the streaming system within one school and explores the perceptions of the pupils within the option process in relation to a number of issues which are raised for the pupils during the process.

My aim is to elucidate how gender, streaming and social class structure the pupils' thinking within the option process, and to consider the implications for the reproduction of gender and social-class relations. Some writers such as Deem (1978), Anyon (1983) and King (1987) have acknowledged the importance of furthering our understanding of the intersections of gender and social class in the education system, but with the notable exception of Riddell (1992) the subject-option process has been rarely approached in this way. Thus, I explore how gender, social class and the streaming system interrelate with each other to structure pupils' perspectives, rather than focusing on a single dimension.

A small subsample of twenty-six pupils (thirteen boys and thirteen girls) was selected for interview from the questionnaire sample. This was a representative subsample in that each 'ability level' was fairly equally present as in the larger sample. The pupils in this subsample were interviewed in depth so as to elicit from them a full account of their reasons for their options and the role of parents, teachers and peers in influencing the option process as they saw it.

Pupils' Reasons for Subject Options

For the twenty-six pupils interviewed it was possible to divide the explicit reasons for subject option into nine different types as shown in Table 18.
The following extracts are examples of each:

Liking for subject — John: top stream; middle-class
I chose physics and chemistry because they're the sort of things I'm interested in. Also I chose technology because I'm interested in electronics, mechanics and computers. I've always been interested in electronics and mechanical things.

Table 18: Reasons given by pupils for subject options

Stream		n	LS	DOS	UC	GA	PAO	LT	DT	DesF	NS
	Boys	4	6	1	9	9	0	2	0	0	0
Top	Girls	4	10	1	5	4	0	0	0	0	0
	Total	8	16	2	14	13	0	2	0	0	0
	Boys	3	3	6	3	1	3	1	1	0	1
Middle	Girls	7	9	7	18	2	7	0	0	0	1
	Total	10	12	13	21	3	10	1	1	0	2
	Boys	6	7	6	4	3	1	2	2	2	1
Bottom	Girls	2	6	2	3	0	0	0	0	1	1
	Total	8	13	8	7	3	1	2	2	3	2
	Boys	13	16	13	16	13	4	5	3	2	2
Totals	Girls	13	25	10	26	6	7	0	0	1	2
	Total	26	41	23	42	19	11	5	3	3	4

Notes: n = number of pupils, LS = Liking for subject opted for, DOS = Dislike for another or other subjects, UC = Usefulness for career, GA = Good ability at subject opted for, PAO = Poor ability at other subjects, LT = Liking for teacher, DT = Dislike for teacher, DesF = Desire to be with friends, NS = New Subject.

Dislike of other subjects — Malcolm: middle stream; middle-class

I chose physics, you know it was a choice between physics and biology [it was compulsory to opt for one science and he had already ruled out chemistry] and I chose physics 'cause I was never much of a biology person.

Usefulness for career — Julie: middle stream

I wanted to do two types of science because at that time I wanted to train to be a nurse.

Good ability at the subject — Philip: bottom stream; working-class

Art, I took that one 'cause the teacher I'd always had seemed not to be able to teach art, but last year I started to progress in it so I decided to keep at art to see if I could turn into Michael Angelo or something.

Poor ability at other subjects — Linda: middle stream

Linda   I chose biology 'cause I'm not that good at physics and I'm not brilliant at maths or anything.

JA   You could have opted for chemistry instead of biology.

Linda   No, I didn't want to do chemistry 'cause it's a bit like physics and it's got all these formulas like maths an' that.

Liking for teachers — Philip: bottom stream; working-class
Did biology 'cause my sister took it and I thought if I got the
same teacher as her it would be alright.

Dislike for teachers — Paul: middle stream; working-class
I opted against chemistry after the first week [of fourth year] because
the teacher gave us a homework on the first night. I thought that
was too much so I dropped it and took up history instead.

Desire to be with friends — Ronnie: bottom stream; working-class

JA   Did you talk to your friends about your choices?
Ronnie Yeah, I talked to me mates before me mum and more
        with them really 'cause we all talked about it together
        so we'd be in the same classes.
JA   Did that actually influence you?
Ronnie Yeah, I think with a couple of them like French. Me
        and David are about the same ability so I made arrange-
        ments with him to see if he wanted to do it. [David and
        Ronnie did, indeed, both opt for French].

New subject — Joseph: middle stream; working-class
I chose technology because it is something new and I could find
things out about it and I wouldn't be behind in it 'cause I haven't
done it before and nobody else had either.

Perceived Ability

Table 18 shows that only pupils in the middle or lower streams opted for
a subject because it was new, that is, a 'minority' subject. Joseph's reason for
choosing technology illustrates how this was related to the sense of failure
felt by middle and lower-stream pupils in the 'main' subjects they were
already studying. By contrast, the top-stream pupils did not feel 'behind'
in 'main' subjects and consequently felt much less inclined to opt out of
them and into new subjects. This partly explains the trends in Table 16.
  Evidently from Table 18 no pupils in the top stream related their
subject options to poor ability in other subjects. Quite the contrary, these
pupils much more than the pupils in the other streams, related their choices
to a past experience of being good at the subjects they study. Middle-
stream pupils particularly mentioned that they had rejected a subject because of poor ability. Furthermore, these pupils rarely claimed to be good
at any school subject. These results support previous research indicating
that the middle-stream pupils as well as the bottom-stream pupils can
experience a great sense of academic failure (Ball, 1981).

Table 19: Pupils' contentment with their place in the streaming system

Stream	n	n_1	n_2	n_3	n_4
Top	53	23(43.4)	10(18.9)	3(5.7)	6(11.3)
Middle	43	22(51.2)	11(25.6)	1(2.3)	11(25.6)
Bottom	27	10(37.0)	2 (7.4)	0(0.0)	2 (7.4)
Totals	123	55(44.7)	23(18.7)	4(3.3)	19(15.4)

Notes:
1 n = number of pupils, n_1 = number of pupils wishing to change at least one class, n_2 = number of pupils wishing to change class for reasons relating to their perceived ability and competition for educational rewards, n_3 = number of pupils wishing to move down the streaming hierarchy, n_4 = number of pupils wishing to move up the streaming hierarchy.
2 Bracketed numbers are percentages of the number of pupils in that stream.

This may be because the middle-stream pupils were still aspiring to succeed academically whereas pupils in the bottom stream had become so disengaged with school knowledge that they had little interest in the academic race. On this point it is interesting that approximately one quarter of the middle-stream pupils from the questionnaire sample wanted to move from some of their classes in order to be *promoted* within the streaming hierarchy because they felt they were failing to achieve (Table 19). For example, Linda described her predicament as follows:

> I'd rather be in a better [meaning higher] English set because I feel I would benefit from it and those in my set are not able to take 'O' level English Lit. because we are presumably [meaning presumed to be] of average ability whereas some of us are better than that.

In some cases these ambitious middle streamers clearly felt distressed about their academic failure relative to the pupils in the top stream. Anita bemoaned:

> I want to be moved up but I am not able to because [already] there are too many [pupils] in the top group [stream]. I feel really bad about this because I have to wait for everyone else.

and Sara complained:

> Want to move up a maths group [stream]. I feel I am being kept back and I want to try to get an 'O' level.

Only two of the twenty-seven bottom-stream pupils expressed feelings of this kind. Thus, the sense of failure generated by pupils' positions in the streaming hierarchy affected how they assessed their 'ability' in subjects. Middle-stream pupils readily assessed their 'ability' as inferior to top-stream pupils and, therefore, poor. As a consequence they readily rejected any subject in which they did not perform well, putting their bad performance down to 'poor ability'. For those middle-stream pupils who, like Anita and Sara, were anxious to obtain high-status qualifications, subjects in which they were able to be allocated to the top stream rather than the middle stream were likely to be much more attractive options. The consequence was that these pupils rejected certain options on the grounds of 'poor ability'.

Since this process was directly related to streaming it was indirectly related to the development of social-class differences since most pupils in the top stream were middle-class and most in the middle stream were working-class. The result is that working-class pupils were much more likely to feel the need to positively reject subjects. Such class division did not require the direct intervention of teachers channelling the middle class into high status 'academic' subjects and the working class into lower-status 'practical' subjects because these pupils had already effectively internalized the school's expectations of their future academic performance as mediated by the streaming system.

Table 18 also shows that, across streams, considerably more boys than girls gave 'good ability' in a subject as a reason for their option. Simultaneously more girls than boys (excepting top-stream pupils) gave 'poor ability' in a subject as their reason for rejecting it. These trends are not explained by the pupils' scores on CATs nor their overall position in the streaming hierarchy. A more likely explanation is sex differences in perceptions of 'ability'. Spender (1980) argues that teachers, consciously or unconsciously, discriminate against girls by expecting less of them than boys, with the consequence that girls learn to underachieve. That argument is supported by the perceptions of the girls in this study. However, my own research did not reveal any clear-cut reasons why girls should be more humble about their ability than boys. In her study of the option process in two comprehensives Riddell found that the way teachers presented equal opportunities to pupils tended to highlight the promising abilities of boys but not girls:

> In general, when the issue of equal opportunities was mentioned, it was in the context of either criticizing girls for their limited horizons or urging boys to move into traditionally female areas where they would soon outstrip their female competitors. This was certainly not an empowering message for the girls who received it. (Riddell, 1992, p. 64)

This might be one explanation for the sex differences in perceived ability at Greenfield. Another might relate to the sex differences in the attention received in classroom interaction (Chapter 5). The social context that the girls perceived was one in which less was expected of them than boys.

Liking/Disliking Subjects and Teachers

Liking and disliking are only superficial explanations for subject options unless we also understand the underlying reasoning. So I asked the pupils what made them like/dislike subjects and teachers in order to gain a greater understanding of the frames of reference which informed the pupils' judgments about subjects. Like Woods (1979) I found that pupils' reasons for likes/dislikes of subjects/teachers took two distinct forms: those that were supportive of the academic value system of the school and those not. The following extracts illustrate this division.

Like for supportive reasons:
Morris: top stream; middle-class.
Mr Pebble's a really good teacher — I've made lots of progress with him.

Dislike for supportive reasons:
Kate: top stream; middle-class.
Didn't like my Spanish teacher 'cause she couldn't teach very well. I don't like teachers who can't control the class. Then everything seems pointless. Her lessons were always chaotic and she's got a record for not getting people through their 'O' levels.

Like for non-supportive reasons:
Michael: bottom stream; working-class.
In computer studies you can't get down to work but you can have a laugh because the teacher can't control the class so you can take advantage. We just generally have a laugh, everyone disrupts the class.

Dislike for non-supportive reasons:
Anne: bottom stream; working-class.
Don't like teachers that have a go at me, separate me from the rest of the class 'cause I'm always talking and then send me to the work centre.

David: bottom stream; working-class.
Don't like CDT 'cause when I walk around the class to get something off a friend, the teacher goes 'Stop walking around! Get to the work centre!'

Nigel: bottom stream; working-class.
Don't like teachers who try to be hard and really bossy like Mr Counter. Counter's always shouting all the time if you miss a homework, he sends a letter home. He walks around the school

Table 20:   *Distribution of supportive and non-supportive pupils*

	Supportive			Non-supportive			
Stream	Boys	Girls	Total	Boys	Girls	Total	Totals
Top	4	3	7	0	1	1	8
Middle	1	4	5	2	3	5	10
Bottom	0	1	1	6	1	7	8
Totals	5	8	13	8	5	13	26

trying to be hard. He has sent me to the work centre about forty times this year.

Clearly there is a sharp contrast between the perspectives of the pupils who gave 'supportive' reasons and those who gave 'non-supportive' reasons. In particular, the 'supportive' pupils were concerned about their academic progress when teachers 'can't control the class'. However, the 'non-supportive' pupils were concerned about the extent to which they were at the sharp end of teachers' rebukes and punishment. The 'non-supportive' pupils frequently mentioned the 'work centre' and concomitantly how they like to 'have a laugh' and 'take advantage' — behaviour which, no doubt, the 'supportive' pupils would define as 'out of control'.

These, then, are two widely differing 'group perspectives' (Woods, 1979) and they are highly correlated with streaming as Table 20 shows. This is further evidence of how streaming structured the perspectives which pupils brought to the option process. In particular, the evidence suggests that 'non-supportive' pupils were inclined to reject subjects which in their experience involved the tightest amount of teacher control because they were likely to associate such subjects with boredom or conflict. Since the high-status 'academic' subjects were the most rigorously examined by teachers who were keen to see their pupils reach high levels of attainment they were likely to be the subjects with the tightest teacher control. Given this, the 'non-supportive' group perspective can be seen as another factor which channelled middle and bottom-stream pupils away from 'academic' subjects and into 'practical' subjects during the option process. Because of the social-class make-ups of the streams this implies that working-class pupils were directed away from 'academic' subjects and towards 'practical' subjects, thus helping to reinforce existing class divisions.

More generally, the 'non-supportive' perspective held predominantly by working-class pupils was a miscalculated evaluation of the worth of subjects as 'academic currency'. Although Willis (1977) stresses how a form of working-class resistance to schooling can underpin that miscalculation, the result in terms of subject options may be further constraints on social choice in the long-term.

Another group perspective which influenced pupils' liking and acceptance of subjects was that of sex roles. This partly explains the sex-polarized trends in science options. There were pro- and anti-science girls. The pro-science girls were mostly in the top stream and opted for two science subjects. A few of these girls had wanted to opt for three 'pure' sciences (biology, chemistry and physics) but the school generally strongly advised boys and girls against this route. The pro-science girls did not sharply distinguish between the sciences.

By contrast, the anti-science girls were mostly in the middle and bottom streams and opted only for one science subject. In general, they drew a sharp distinction between biology and the other science subjects. The subject-preference questionnaire revealed that mathematics was particularly unpopular amongst these girls. Some of the girls in M3 told the teacher directly that mathematics was a 'boy's subject'. Significantly, the anti-science girls stated that they did not like physics and chemistry for reasons such as 'it's got all these formulas like maths an' that or 'there are too many boring equations'. Biology was contrasted with the rest of science:

> Did biology 'cause if you wanna do something to do with children
> you wanna know about the body instead of all science experiments.

Furthermore, these girls consistently related their preference for biology to traditionally feminine roles such as nursing, mothering or cooking. As Measor (1983) found, these anti-science girls seemed to be using their preferences to negotiate their gender identities.

The boys tended to opt for an additional technological subject such as technology or CDT in preference to biology. Some of the boys clearly opted in this way because they believed CDT and technology were boys' subjects.

> **JA** Why do you think boys get more attention in CDT and PE?
>
> **David** Because they're doing something like football or rugby but with childcare or typing or home economics girls get more attention because it's their kind of subject.
>
> **JA** Why do you say it's their kind of subject?
>
> **David** Because women do the cooking it's a girl's subject whereas with CDT you don't see a woman working in a factory at technology you see a man so it's a boy's subject or a man's subject. You don't have a woman CDT teacher you have a man and you don't have a man teacher for cooking you have a woman.

Like David, many of the other boys avoided 'girls' subjects'. As with the anti-science girls these boys drew on roles, but this time masculine ones,

Table 21: *Distribution of career/occupational expectations of girls across streams*

Stream	Mf	Mn	NMf	NMm	NMn	DK	Totals
Top	0	0	7	5	3	11	26
Middle	6	0	8	2	5	13	34
Bottom	2	1	2	2	2	4	13
Totals	8	1	17	9	10	28	73

Notes: Mf = Manual and feminine, Mn = Manual and neutral, NMf = Non-Manual and feminine, NMm = Non-Manual and masculine, NMn = Non-Manual and neutral, DK = Don't Know.

Table 22: *Distribution of career/occupational expectations of boys across streams*

Stream	Mm	NMm	NMn	DK	Totals
Top	0	19	5	3	27
Middle	3	1	2	3	9
Bottom	8	0	0	6	14
Totals	11	20	7	12	50

such as doctor, electrician, and working with electronics and mechanical things, to justify their choices into physical science and technological subjects. Such group perspectives, therefore, facilitate knowledge-culture polarization along gender and class dimensions.

Career Expectations

Pupils were asked what they would like to do when they left school. Many had no clear ideas about their future careers but the responses of those who had were analysed. Most, though not all could be categorized into a 'manual/non-manual' divide using the socio-economic categorizations of the Office of Population Censuses and Surveys. Where the pupil aspired to some form of higher education (e.g., university) his or her career expectation was classified as non-manual. Career expectations were also classified along a 'feminine'/'masculine'/'neutral' divide according to whether the job or career in question was traditionally associated with 'women's work', 'men's work' or neither. Aspirations to higher education were regarded as neutral unless a particular subject or vocational training was mentioned.

Tables 21 and 22 show that most top and middle-stream pupils aspired to 'non-manual' careers. Bottom-stream boys, in particular, wanted only 'manual' jobs with the exception of one. These tables show a positive relationship between streaming and career expectation similar to, but not the same as, that between streaming and social class. Whilst the two relationships coincide for the top stream (predominantly middle-class and 'non-manual' career aspirations) and the bottom stream (predominantly

Table 23: Association between career expectations of girls and subject options

Career			Subject Type			
Expectation	Academic	Practical	Feminine	Masculine	Neutral	Totals
Mf	30	16	25	3	18	46
Mn	2	3	3	0	2	5
NMf	77	25	45	13	44	102
NMm	43	12	17	15	23	55
NMn	44	18	24	11	27	62

Table 24: Association of career expectations of boys and subject options

Career			Subject Type			
Expectation	Academic	Practical	Feminine	Masculine	Neutral	Totals
Mm	36	21	13	23	21	57
NMm	100	18	21	49	48	118
NMn	28	12	7	13	20	40

working-class and 'manual' career aspirations) this is not the case for the middle stream (predominantly working-class but 'non-manual' career aspirations). Thus, if the pupils' career aspirations were to be realized then a simple reproduction of social-class relations would not occur.

Similarly, Table 22 shows that a considerable proportion of the girls (43 per cent) of those who gave a career expectation) aspire to non-manual 'masculine' or 'neutral' careers. Were these aspirations to be realized then changes in, rather than the reproduction of, gender relations within the occupational structure would occur. The boys' aspirations, however, tell a very different story. Not one boy in the whole sample could be categorized as aspiring to a traditionally 'feminine' career. If the aspirations of the boys in this sample were to be realized then existing gender relations would probably be reinforced along traditional lines. These results confirm the large-scale survey research of Lueptow (1981).

Insofar as pupils' career aspirations affected their actual subject options they ceased to be dreams about the future and began to shape the real choices these adolescents would have later in life. As Herzog puts it:

> before young women and men have ever entered a full-time job and faced the constraints of the labour market, they have already 'lined up' for different kinds of jobs. (Herzog, 1982, p. 10)

Tables 23 and 24 indicate that the career aspirations of the boys and girls did indeed positively affect subject options. Pupils who wanted 'manual' occupations opted for proportionally many more 'practical' subjects than did the pupils aspiring to 'non-manual' occupations. Also while girls generally opted for proportionally more feminine subjects than masculine subjects, the subset of girls aspiring to 'masculine' occupations opted for almost as many 'masculine' subjects as 'feminine' ones (Table 23). Similarly, the boys aspiring to 'masculine' occupations opted for proportionally many more 'masculine' subjects than the boys aspiring to 'neutral' occupations (Table 24).

Interviews substantiated that career expectations were not only correlated with types of subject option but that they were a major *causative* factor (Table 18). These results suggest a further factor which causes working-class pupils to opt into 'practical' subjects and boys into 'masculine' subjects. Such options represent a first step in the reproduction of the dominant social class and gender relations.

Given a pupil's career aspiration, it is not only the pupil's beliefs about appropriate subjects which influence his or her option. Parental intervention can be an important factor in structuring the pupil's beliefs about the appropriateness of a subject. Before considering some examples of the importance of parental intervention in the process it is useful to gain a greater understanding of its nature and extent for the pupils interviewed.

I used Woods' categories of 'strong guidance', 'mutual resolution', 'reassurance' and 'little or nil' to describe different types of parental consultation. Strong guidance was characterized by a heavy dose of narrow parental advice in a certain direction which the pupil felt reluctant to go in but eventually acquiesced.

Kerry: top stream; middle-class
JA   Why did you take French?

Kerry I didn't want to take that but my dad told me I ought to do it.

JA   So you obviously discussed it with your parents. Was it a lengthy discussion?

Kerry Not very long. I didn't discuss physics, chemistry and all that lot with them but I had one option left and I didn't want to take French. We just discussed that.

Mutual resolution was typical of pupils who were rather unsure about certain choices and wanted to discuss their uncertainty with parents willing to do so.

Jeremy: middle stream; working-class
JA   Did you discuss it [subject choice] with your parents?

Jeremy Yeah.

JA   What sort of advice did they have?

Jeremy They asked me what I wanted to do when I left school and looked at my subjects and said 'that's a good idea' 'cause they all sort of interlocked.

Table 25a: Types of parental consultation

Stream	Little or Nil	Reassurance	Mutual Resolution	Strong Guidance	Totals
Top	1	1	4	2	8
Middle	1	6	2	1	10
Bottom	2	5	0	1	8
Totals	4	12	6	4	26

Table 25b: Extent of parental consultation

Stream	None	Brief	Detailed	Totals
Top	1	2	5	8
Middle	1	6	3	10
Bottom	2	5	1	8
Totals	4	13	9	26

JA	How long would you say you discussed it for?
Jeremy	Dunno exactly.
JA	Just one evening?
Jeremy	Oh no, more times than that. When they come home from work they'd discuss it with me.
JA	How long did this go on for?
Jeremy	About a week.

Typically with 'reassurance' the pupil merely showed choices made to his or her parents who approved without taking any part in moulding the decision.

Mary: middle stream

JA	How long did you spend discussing it [subject choice] with your parents?
Mary	Not long, about a quarter of an hour. I chose it first and then I asked them what they thought and my mum said as long as I'd chosen for what I wanted to do when I'd left school that was O.K.. My dad said the same really.

Finally, a few pupils had no consultation with their parents at all about subject options.

Tables 25a and 25b show that middle-class parents made a much greater intervention in their pupils' option decision. 75 per cent of the top-stream pupils interviewed received either 'strong guidance' or reached a 'mutual resolution'. By contrast, working-class parents tended to be much less involved in the whole process and only 30 per cent and 12.5 per cent of the middle and bottom-stream pupils respectively fell into the categories of 'strong guidance' or 'mutual resolution'. Similarly, the extent of the parental advice received by most top-stream pupils tended to be much more detailed than that received by most middle and bottom-stream pupils. This evidence suggests that working-class pupils were more likely to opt according to their own aspirations (career or otherwise) while middle-class pupils were more likely to find themselves directed away from options considered inappropriate by their parents. In particular, this evidence suggests that the predominantly working-class 'non-supportive' pupils were unlikely to have their miscalculations 'corrected' by parental intervention.

Gender was also found to play an important part in affecting the nature of parental advice. The typing option serves to illustrate this well. Many of the middle and bottom-stream girls had opted for typing yet frequently it was their least favourite subject. In fact, many of these girls seemed to have chosen typing as a skill to fall back on if they failed to get any other kind of job. This was a view that clearly some parents encouraged for their daughters.

Anne: bottom stream; working-class
Anne   Well, I chose typing 'cause if you get a job typing gets you somewhere. Gets you a job or something like a secretary an' that.
JA   Did you talk to your parents about it?
Anne   They said 'Do typing 'cause it gets you somewhere' and I was interested in typing anyway.

Sandra: middle stream
Sandra   . . . And typing — God knows why.
JA   Why do you say that?
Sandra   Well, I think my mum chose that really so that if I don't get a job straight away I'll be able to use it. But it's really boring.

Thus, the parents of the middle and bottom-stream girls choosing typing did not try to dissuade their daughters from opting for typing, but positively encouraged it. However, the one working-class boy who wished to take typing experienced quite different parental advice.

Philip: bottom stream; working-class
Philip   At first I was gonna do typing then decided on technology.
JA   Why did you change your mind?
Philip   Well I thought I'd be the only boy doing it and my dad had a bit of a laugh at me about it.
JA   What did your dad say?

Philip He said that it's only a girl's subject, typing. I try to argue with him but never get anywhere with him.
JA Did your mates influence you?
Philip They didn't really influence me. But there wouldn't be any of my mates in typing. I'd be sitting in typing with a load of girls and a teacher and that would be boring.

While the working-class girls' mothers advised their daughters to opt for typing, Philip's working-class father advised against it on the grounds that it was 'only a girls' subject'. The views of Philip's father reveal that he believed typing was inappropriate for boys and of low status because it was a 'girls' subject'. Here the subject-option process tended to reinforce dominant gender relations within the working-class occupational sphere. As the responses of Anne and Sandra indicate, it is important to appreciate that this takes place in the context of socio-economic pressures. The economic insecurity of working-class parents partly explains their advice. Typing was seen as a marketable skill for girls but not for boys.

Peer Pressure

Although Philip denied that his mates influenced his rejection of typing as an option, he also mentioned peer-pressure factors such as 'there wouldn't be any of my mates in typing'. Table 18 shows that the 'desire to be with friends' was not a major factor in causing the pupils to opt *into* subjects. However, this category is rather limited as an indicator of the impact of peer pressure on the option process because, as was the case with Philip 'desire to be with friends' can cause a pupil to opt *out* of a certain subject. The following example illustrates that peer pressure can have a powerful impact on pupil subject choice even if it does not determine the final option.

Jenny: middle stream
JA Did you talk to your parents about your choice?
Jenny Yeah, 'cause I was gonna do typing and my mum said, 'Well don't, do French instead' and she'd teach me how to type. My dad agreed.
JA Why were you going to do typing?
Jenny 'Cause all the girls are doing it. I don't think there's hardly any girls not doing typing, only about four. [In fact, very few top-stream girls took typing]. They ask you 'Why aren't you doing typing?' in a very surprised manner like that.
JA Did you discuss your choice with your friends?

Jenny   Yeah, but they said 'Do typing' but my dad's friends said French is more important.

JA   Are you regretting not doing typing?

Jenny   Well I am in a way 'cause French I have to work hard at it all the time.

JA   You've said that you want to change into typing?

Jenny   Well, yeah, after the first few weeks in French I wanted to change out of French and into typing but I wasn't allowed. It was, well in French most of my friends I'd been with for a long time and suddenly they weren't there but I can cope now.

Clearly Jenny experienced a great deal of peer pressure to 'do typing' even to the point where she rejected her parents' advice.

Peer pressure from boys can also cause girls to dislike male-dominated subjects. This can be particularly powerful. Alison had opted for technology. She was the only girl out of the seventy-three girls who responded to my subject-option questionnaire to do so, and the only girl in her fourth-year technology class. She came to 'hate' her technology classes because some of the boys in the class called her 'a slag' and victimized her.

JA   Why don't you like technology classes?

Alison Well, I used to hate it and the boys in the class were really nasty to me because I was the only girl in the class.

JA   How were they nasty to you?

Alison They'd call me a slag. If I sat at one end of the room, they'd all get up and move or something. All jokes were directed at me.

JA   Did that upset you a lot?

Alison Yeah, it did.

JA   Did it stop you working?

Alison Yeah, I was thinking about giving it [technology] up and my mum said that it might be a good idea.

JA   Do you know any other girls who have similar problems?

Alison I know another who is the only girl in the CDT class. She says that the whole class ignore her totally but don't call her names.

JA   Did these boys call you any other names?

Alison Well, they used to say the only reason I was doing technology was because it was the only chance I'd got to get near any boys.

JA   What did the teacher used to do?

Alison Nothing. He didn't know how to handle it. It wasn't just telling someone off for a normal reason.

101

Alison's account was substantiated by consulting her school record and by a discussion with the deputy headteacher who was aware of the problem. In fact, due to directed teacher intervention, the situation improved for Alison and she did not give up studying technology. Nevertheless, this illustrates yet another way in which gender and sexism structures pupil peer pressure which in turn affects the pupil's subject option. Furthermore, other girls heard about Alison's experiences just as she had heard about another girl's difficulties in CDT. Insofar as these girls were considering the option of studying technology in the future, Alison's experience can only have been a deterrent. Hence, such sexist peer pressure indirectly serves to maintain gender-polarized subject options, especially when effective teacher intervention is slow and faltering. Alison's case illustrates the problem that boys' sexism creates in the classroom if the teacher does not have a clear anti-sexist pedagogy. Without such a pedagogy sexism, as Alison sensed, is not seen as a serious form of misbehaviour.

Conclusion

The teachers and the school presented themselves as progressive about equal opportunities for boys and girls. They saw themselves as having to cope with the traditional beliefs of pupils and parents that led to a gender-based knowledge culture polarization. My research suggests that that was only a half-truth. Peer pressure was usually a conservative force, encouraging pupils to remain in groups defined by the dominant gender and 'ability' order. Working-class parental intervention also tended to have a gender conservative effect.

Other research which has examined parents' perspectives on school subjects and careers for their children has also revealed considerable support for traditional gender divisions (Riddell, 1992). However, there was some dissension from traditional social class and gender relations at Greenfield. That is reflected by some middle-class girls striving for high-status masculine careers, and by those working-class middle-stream pupils who wished to move up the streaming hierarchy to obtain middle-class jobs and career opportunities. Moreover, this chapter reveals that the school's organizational differentiation affected knowledge culture polarization. This issue strikes at the heart of the 'ideology of free choice' that has pervaded the subject-option process in many comprehensives (Riddell, 1992, p. 53). For pupils' subject options are structured by their perceived abilities and identification with the norms of teachers and the school.

The foregoing analysis indicates that policies designed to eliminate or reduce the reproduction of social class and gender relations cannot be unidimensional. Efforts made by official bodies to encourage girls into science are likely to have little impact on the 'non-supportive' girls because they and their parents are so dislocated from the schooling process through a history of being labelled as failures. Insofar as a 'girls into science' policy is effective for the 'supportive' girls, it will still have little impact on the class-related 'practical'–'academic' divide, and consequently little impact on class divisions in wider society.

Chapter 7

Gendering and Stratification of School Knowledge

For pupils the school day is split up into 'packets' of time (periods) in which they are expected to engage with different knowledge-systems (subjects). At Greenfield there were seven periods per day, each forty or forty-five minutes long. Each fourth year had five English and five mathematics periods per week and the pupils taking French had four periods of it per week. The combination of fragmenting pupils' time and space in the school day and dividing their experience of school knowledge was fundamental to the organization of the school. The school staff were specialists in certain subjects and they were collected into subject-based departments which took responsibility for the teaching of certain knowledge systems.

In general, the relationship between experience and 'knowledge' is a complex one. However, in the case of school knowledge, pupil experience is rigidly structured. Society rules that schooling is compulsory and schools insist that lesson attendance is compulsory. Teachers in classrooms are empowered with certain sanctions which they can bring to bear on pupils refusing to conform to the classroom rules and conventions. The power relationships between community, schools, classroom teachers and pupils are, therefore, fundamental to the controlling of pupil experience *vis-à-vis* school knowledge.

School knowledge is a form of packaged experiences, social conventions and traditions. It is a cultural, as well as an organizational, phenomenon. But school knowledge is not just any old package of experiences, conventions and traditions; it is directed into subjects and, concomitantly, subject boundaries. Some theoretical ideas put forward by Bernstein (1971) can help us think about the nature of this packaging. In Bernstein's terms the English, mathematics and French curricula in Greenfield Comprehensive stood in a 'closed' relation to each other. These subjects were well insulated from each other and no attempt was being made to integrate them. There was a strong boundary between the curriculum contents of each of these subjects, that is, there was strong classification.

Given this, pupils' experience across these subjects was extremely compartmentalized. Although all three were academic, pupils may be forgiven for thinking that they were being asked to engage in three separate, academic learning processes. Consequently, pupils exhibited different responses to these subjects and we know from foregoing discussions that this had some gender basis. In this chapter I shall describe the character- istics of the three subjects at Greenfield and discuss how gender and class- related differentiation occurred within them. To do this I focus on the stratification and gendering of school knowledge.

The issue of stratification of school knowledge was first raised in the sociology of education by Young (1971) and developed by Bourdieu (1973) and others. In secondary schools stratification is directly linked to teachers' assumptions about 'ability', and this is where the relationship between streaming and knowledge stratification becomes evident.

Interest in how men and women are represented in language and texts has grown as a result of feminist research into sexism in social relations (Deem, 1978; Delamont, 1990). I refer to such sex-related representation as the gendering of language and texts. The rationale for studying sexism in language has been largely derived from the arguments of Sapir (1970) and Whorf (1956) that the nature of language influences and structures, if not determines, social relations. Consequently, feminists concerned to challenge sexism in society have begun to question and challenge hitherto accepted forms of sexism in language and discourse (Kenway *et al.*, 1994; Martyna, 1980; Spender, 1980).

There is now a considerable literature pointing to sexist gendering in school texts and curriculum materials. In English-subject schoolbooks, reading schemes and picture books, research has consistently found that texts are male-dominated, and that the activities and roles of characters in the texts are rigidly dichotomized and stereotyped along sex lines (Davies, and Meighan, 1975; Lobban, 1975; Montieth, 1979). Similar findings have been reported concerning mathematics, physics and chemistry textbooks (Northam, 1982; Berrill and Wallis, 1976; Taylor, 1979; Walford, 1980; 1981). However, one limitation of these textual analyses is that they tend to have been carried out in isolation from other aspects of the schooling process. One advantage of my ethnographic case-study approach is that it is possible to contextualize gendering of school texts in terms of school organization and teacher ideology (Chapter 8). Another limitation of the isolated textual analyses is that they can neglect subject differences which arise out of the ways texts are utilized within different subject cultures.

Mathematics

In mathematics I found that setting determined the pacing of work through the subject as mediated by the pupils' textbooks. Each set that I observed used a different textbook. The mathematical knowledge within them was 'stratified' in the sense that it contained a ranking tailored to the examina- tion system. Following Bernstein (1971) we might say that the knowledge was strongly framed. For example, the authors of M1's textbook *Simple*

Modern Maths 3 (SMM3) (Court and Court, 1980) made a 'note to teachers' saying:

> This book has been written for pupils taking CSE and O level examinations. It includes a large range of both modern and traditional topics to enable it to be used with a wide variety of syllabuses. One of the difficulties found in using a series of books is that in the final year of the course much of the work that needs to be revised is in the earlier books. This difficulty has been overcome in this book by the inclusion of revision exercises. This makes Book 3 a complete final course for CSE and O level. It is suggested that when preparing for examinations, past papers should be worked through in addition to revising from this book.

Compare this with the equivalent 'note to teachers' in M5's textbook *Simple Modern Maths 1* (Boyde, *et al.*) (1976):

> This book has been written for pupils who find mathematics difficult but who want to take CSE. Books 1 and 2 together cover the main concepts required for CSE examinations. Many of the examples are very easy and the non-examination pupil will also find the book useful. As far as possible all the Units contain examples of the practical application of the topics so that pupils can see the relevance of mathematics to everyday life.

It was well known that CSE qualifications were of lower status than 'O' level ones. Schoolwork for CSEs was defined as *easier*, not just different. Thus, the mathematics textbooks acted as powerful mediating agents of knowledge differentiation.

For the topic 'Area and Volume' M5's textbook included examples of finding the areas of rectangular and triangular shapes plus the surface area and volume of cuboids. In a separate section finding the area of a circle was also included. Area was explained by the counting of the number of squares covered by shapes. The M3 textbook, *Integrated Maths Scheme* (IMS) approached area via the trapezium. Calculating the area of the trapezium could involve studying the area of triangles and rectangles. It also introduced the idea of using trapeziums to approximate areas under curves. By contrast. M1's textbook included exercises in the area of the triangle, parallelogram, trapezium, circle, sectors, segments and the volumes of prisms, cylinders, pyramids, cones, frustrums of cones and spheres. Surface areas of cylinders, cones and spheres were also mentioned.

The same trend followed for most other topics and most *topics* were common to all three textbooks. The M1 textbook took most topics further thus making more connections with other substantive topics. The topic of 'sets and Venn diagrams' was a good example of this. M1's textbook was the only one to make explicit reference to the relationship between sets and logic and to establish the properties of sets by proof. Whatever the pupils in the three sets actually did, their textbooks made available vastly different areas of mathematical knowledge. Of course, the teachers were aware of these differences in the approach to knowledge. Indeed it informed their practice.

Classroom observation established that mathematics lessons followed a similar pattern of stratification. All the lessons in mathematics tended to be structured around the topics in the textbook although the teachers frequently used examples not to be found in the textbook. Nevertheless, these examples reflected those given in the textbook and did not in themselves open up any new topic of mathematical enquiry. In my very first observation lesson with M5 the teacher whispered to me as I sat down: 'this is the bottom group so it's [the mathematics] a bit limited'. The lesson was on ratio and it mirrored the approach in the textbook under the topic 'sharing things out'. The teacher changed the examples from, say, running a pop festival to setting up a car business and substituted fictional names for names of pupils in the class. I am not arguing that this was poor teaching given the paradigm purpose within which the teacher was working. Clearly his aim was to give the pupils a break from the textbook and motivate them by involving them in the examples. I merely wish to point out that the *boundaries of stratification* are not changed by this procedure and that my observational research data suggests that the textbook was a strong knowledge differentiator in fourth-year school mathematics.

Thus, school mathematics was stratified along a clearly defined continuum of 'easy' to 'less easy' to 'difficult' both within and between textbooks. This was possible because school mathematics was packaged as a cumulative subject. It has also been presented in this way in the mathematics curriculum-development rhetoric (Cockcroft, 1982). According to this view, the 'difficult' problems in mathematics may only be tackled when the 'fundamental' problems have been mastered. Mr Bird, the teacher of M1, explained to his class when referring to the imminent fourth-year exam how the stratification of school mathematics is reflected in the examination papers. He told the pupils that the level 3 paper was for the top set, but that level 2 was for 'CSE people and *therefore* it *has* to be a much easier paper' (my emphasis). This comment served to remind the top-set pupils that they were attempting more difficult and more challenging mathematical work which was beyond the capability of pupils in lower sets.

This strict stratification was highlighted by an incident that occurred when I administered a questionnaire to M3. One of the questions asked the pupils to estimate how they thought they would perform in their end of fourth-year exams. One pupil asked the teacher, Ms Frost, if they (the M3 set) were 'allowed' to get better than grade 3. Ms Frost explained to her that because the M3 pupils would be taking CSE (rather than 'O' level) that a grade 3 was, in fact, the highest they could score. This illustrated how the academic value system of the school was rigidly and positively related to the examination status which was, in turn, positively related to the stratified knowledge.

By focusing on stratification I have emphasized the differences between the mathematics sets but there were some important similarities. In the first instance little or no group work was encouraged in any of the lessons that I observed. In M1 and M5 I found that the teacher tried to enforce *individual* working. In the case of M1, Mr Bird had a strong preference that the pupils sat in the same seats each lesson and he often required the pupils to work in silence. The pupils were seated in pairs forming rows. In some lessons the teacher sat behind his desk and pupils were expected to bring their problems up to him individually. The teacher then discussed problems with the individual pupil at his desk. It was during these times that the rest of the class might lapse into discussion. On such occasions Mr Bird would insist that the pupils work at their questions (from the textbook) without discussion.

In M5 Mr Counter allowed the pupils to sit where they wanted within the limits of the rowed pairs of desks structuring the classroom. For example, at the beginning of one lesson David was separated from Ronnie and Michael for trying to sit with them in a threesome. Mr Counter was more liberal than Mr Bird about the noise level allowed in his class but no movement between desks by pupils during the class was permitted without rebuke unless there was 'good reason' in the teacher's eyes. In M3 walking around the class without explanation to the teacher sometimes went without comment but at other times was rebuked. This rather inconsistent stance on the part of Ms Frost left her open to pupil discontent. Often pupils would be discussing a party that they had attended the previous night or some incident unrelated to school mathematics but sometimes they would help each other with their work and Ms Frost did not always know which. Consequently, pupils would complain about being rebuked for working.

The individualistic philosophy which dominated the mathematics classroom was partly related to how the project of learning mathematics was perceived. Although the 'discipline' preferred by the teacher was also an important factor, the fact that mathematics was seen almost entirely as a quest for the right answer to be found by applying formulae also seemed crucial. That is, the 'algorithmic view' of mathematics, in which 'the subject is seen as a collection of algorithms for solving various problems, and the practice of mathematics is seen as matching problem to algorithm' (Bibby, 1983). I found that this approach to mathematics was actively encouraged, especially in M1. The following four examples illustrate the point.

Example 1: Lesson notes for M1
The class is working quietly on approximating a solution by graphical work. From behind his desk the teacher decides to see what answers the pupils have got. A few people call out numbers in the top 30s and bottom 40s. The teacher informs the class that they are supposed to obtain an answer of about 41.9. Matthew says he has got 83 point something. The teacher instantly cuts him off in a loud voice 'What?' (not expecting an answer) as soon as Matthew gets 83 out. Charlotte then puts up her hand to say that she got '280 or something'. The teacher's expression is disbelief. He says 'How did you get that dear? Well there's no answer to that is there.' Rest of the class is laughing.

Although it was coming near to the end of the lesson there was still time for the teacher to explore some of the reasons for the *wrong* answers.

Example 2: Lesson notes for M1
At the end of the lesson teacher says 'All stand.' This instructs all the pupils to stand behind their desks to wait to be dismissed. The teacher then goes around the class asking pupils individually for the formula of the roots of a quadratic equation. Pupils who get it right are allowed to go. Those who get the wrong answer are not dismissed. Eventually everyone is dismissed.

This was a sort of game which the teacher played with M1 on the odd occasion at the end of a lesson. Nevertheless it emphasized the importance of getting the right answer. Right answers were rewarded and wrong answers were ignored or dismissed.

Example 3: Lesson notes from M1
In rebuking one pupil's activity in class, Mr Bird told the class: 'You don't revise by reading but by doing — you know that in maths.'

The clear implication is that mathematics is not a subject to be read about and discussed but rather it is to be persistently practised until speedy and comprehensive manipulation of the available algorithms is achieved, ready for the examinations.

Example 4: Lesson notes from staffroom
On another occasion some of the maths teachers in the staffroom showed concern that a cumulative frequency question in an 'O' level mathematics paper contained the word 'decile' rather than the more familiar notions of quartile and percentile. The teachers were concerned because they had not introduced the word decile

and thought that some of their pupils might be thrown into confusion by it appearing on the exam paper.

The word did not fit the algorithm. Pupils do, however, spend a lot of
time working in tens with decimals but these are different algorithms. The
imaginative step from *decimal* to *decile* apparently was not expected of
mathematics pupils. This might well be a realistic assessment, but the
assumption illustrates the extent and closure of the algorithmic approach.
Even *within* mathematics, algorithms often stand in a closed relationship
to each other. Knowledge is sharply compartmentalized in order to be
quickly recalled and fitted to the appropriate problems.

   If a pupil is competent in selecting his or her algorithms to fit the
problems then he or she can get the right answer without discussion.
Hence the greater the competence of the pupil the greater the chance of the
individualistic learning philosophy being successful for the teacher. By
giving the less competent pupils problems which require a lesser reper-
toire of algorithms the textbooks contribute to such individualism. Simultaneously these pupils do not have the algorithms to fit the more difficult
problems and are labelled as less able to perform school mathematics.
Thus, the stratified school mathematics textbooks which serve a stratified
examination system based on individualistic philosophy feed the algorithmic approach which, in turn, creates a pedagogical relationship amenable
to an individualistic learning philosophy. In this way stratification of school
knowledge has a central impact on pedagogy.

   The following example illustrates the impact of the 'algorithmic'
perspective on the learning process. The teacher of M3 had provided
everyone with a sheet of formulae giving the area of various shapes. As
a revision exercise the class was instructed to work through the examples
on this sheet using the appropriate formulae. For some of the lesson I sat
with Alice. She was trying to find the area of a circle using $A = \pi r^2$ given
the information that the diameter was 12 cm. She wrote

$$A = \pi \times 12 \times 12$$

Alice Is that right?

JA   You've written $A = \pi$ times the diameter squared but the
          radius is only half the diameter (pointing to the equation
          on the sheet $d = 2r$).

Alice Oh, so I have to half it (meaning the area).
          (She divides her previous answer by two and appears
          convinced that she has the right answer.)

JA   You've halved the area not the diameter. It's the radius
          which is half the *diameter*.

Alice Oh, so the radius is 6. So, ah, it's a circle half the size of
          the one with diameter 12.

JA   No, it's the same circle as that. That's the circle you're
trying to find the area of.
(At this stage Alice looked completely blank. I drew some
diagrams of the circles marking the radii and diameters of
the required circle and the one for which she had origi-
nally calculated the area. After this she seemed to understand where she had gone wrong.)

Alice illustrates a couple of points. First, her immediate anxiety about
having the right answer gives away the main point of the project of doing
mathematics for her. One practises formulae to get right answers. And
secondly, when she could not get the right answer her strategy was to
search for another algorithm like . . . 'and now divide your answer by
two' rather than try to understand the problem or even consider the point
of doing this problem.

Mathematics was a particularly unpopular subject amongst the pupils
in my sample. It was especially unpopular with a fraction of the girls.
Almost one quarter of the girls in my sample stated that it was their least
favourite subject. For pupils in the bottom set the stratification of mathematics reinforced their perceived lack of ability by the school. In an M5
class Eric called out: 'Sir, I could do those questions when I was a 10-year-
old!' Shaking his head, he continued: 'What's the point of that?' Ronnie
(S[2] = 10) voiced similar feelings:

JA   What do you think about the textbooks you use in
maths?
Ronnie Maths, at the beginning it's embarrassing to look at
them 'cause it's got so easy questions in it. Baby questions in it at first.

Another reason why mathematics was particularly unpopular was the
pupils' frustration with not being able to obtain the right answers. Since
right answers were ascribed such importance in mathematics failing to
obtain them was seen to imply to the pupils that their efforts were fruit-
less. Often the response of the pupils was to think that they might be in
too high a set for mathematics:

JA   You say you find maths difficult?
Kate   Yeah, I don't know why I'm in the 'top' set really.

This response indicates the close linkage between getting right answers and the way the mathematics curriculum is stratified by the setting
system. Thus, any attempt to reduce the stratification of school mathematics does face some qualitatively specific problems such as finding
basic alternatives to the dominant algorithmic perspective (Abraham and

Table 26: Crude quantitative analysis of maths textbooks

Textbook	Class	Males	Females
SMM3	M1	50	38
IMS	M3	35	22
SMM1	M5	107	40
Totals		192	100

Bibby, 1988; 1989). In many other subjects such as English, history, geography and humanities, major alternatives to the algorithmic perspective already exist.

During my research I found that the gendering of mathematical knowledge was widespread *across* sets. Given the importance of textbooks in mathematics, I carried out a textual analysis of the three main mathematics textbooks used by M1, M3 and M5. All examples in which males or females were involved in the mathematical problem were counted. Subexamples were counted as the same single example unless questions concerning the opposite sex to the one introduced in the main example appeared (Table 26). I also took a note of all the male and female 'real-life agency' included in examples. This excluded certain activities which conveyed no context in which gender could be significant in identifying with the activity. For example, a man walking at a certain relative velocity to a moving train would be included in the crude content of examples including males but excluded from male 'real-life agency'. By contrast, a woman shopping for a washing machine would be included as 'real-life agency'.

A similar, though not identical analysis was carried out for the French textbooks. The selected cases of 'real-life agency' were then organized into the following categories:

(a) Playing football/rugby/cricket
(b) Playing tennis/hockey
(c) Playing other sports (e.g., men having a 'tug-of-war')
(d) Doing metalwork/woodwork
(e) Doing needlework
(f) Analysis of employment/analysis of income
(g) Betting
(h) Cooking
(i) Buying/making/selling domestic goods (i.e., food, kitchenware, flowers)
(j) Buying/selling/making non-domestic goods
(k) Adventurous outdoor activities (e.g., rockclimbing, skiing)
(l) Running a concern (e.g., business, investment, pop festival)
(m) Police officer/fire officer/customs officer/doctor/teacher/director/student/mathematician

(n) Burglars/bank robbers/criminals
(o) Farmer/gamekeeper/hunter/labourer/bricklayer/carpenter/
     driver/builder/haulage contractor/furniture remover/chauf-
     feur
(p) Grocer/shopkeeper/trader/insurer/sales representative/wine-
     taster/commercial traveller/dealer
(q) Reporter/interviewer
(r) Fashion designer/designer/manufacturer
(s) Fashion model
(t) Air host (ess)/wait (ress)
(u) Typist/telephonist
(v) Fortune teller
(w) Photographer
(x) Perfume maker

My results (Table 27) support and complement Northam's (1982) study of primary-maths books for the age range 3–13 years. The textbooks I analysed were found to be extremely male-dominated. Moreover, male and female agency was extremely stereotyped. There were many more males represented in active roles. Women tended to be shopping for food or buying washing machines, whilst men tended to be running businesses or investing. Almost every occupation mentioned in the mathematics textbooks was assumed to be masculine, even mathematician! *Simple Modern Maths 1* was sexist to the point of being factually incorrect when it stated:

> If the government says that the unemployment rate is 6 per cent they mean that averaged over the whole country, 6 out of every 100 *men* are unemployed. (Court and Court, 1980, p. 84, my emphasis)

Also in the sections on income tax, men were represented as the financial 'heads' of household. It was always a 'man and his wife' and never a 'woman and her husband'. The category 'single man' was used but never 'single woman'. The car dealer was male while the woman sold her car. Boys did woodwork but girls did cooking and needlework although one mixed cooking class was mentioned. Sport was also stereotyped. In short, the activities which made up the 'background' to many mathematics examples were heavily gendered.

This type of analysis, however, does not tell us much about the effect of such gendering on pupils. In my interviews with the pupils several boys and girls told me directly that in mathematics and physics the illustrations and examples nearly always involved men rather than women. Some others said that they did not think about it. None of the

Table 27: Real-life agency analysis of mathematics and French textbooks

| | Texts | | | | | | | | | | | | |
| | SMM1 | | IMS | | SMM3 | | B3 | | B4 | | NNN | | Totals | |
Categories	M	F	M	F	M	F	M	F	M	F	M	F	M	F
(a)	2	0	1	0	1	0	0	0	0	0	0	0	4	0
(b)	0	0	0	1	0	2	0	0	0	0	0	0	0	3
(c)	0	0	0	1	0	3	0	0	0	0	0	0	0	4
(d)	2	0	0	0	0	0	0	0	0	0	0	0	2	0
(e)	0	1	0	0	0	0	0	0	0	0	0	0	0	1
(f)	4	0	0	0	2	0	0	0	0	0	0	0	6	0
(g)	1	0	0	0	0	0	0	0	0	0	0	0	1	0
(h)	1	3	0	0	0	0	0	1	0	0	0	0	1	4
(i)	0	6	1	1	0	3	0	0	0	0	0	1	1	11
(j)	6	1	0	0	0	1	2	0	0	0	0	0	8	2
(k)	2	0	1	0	0	0	7	2	0	0	2	0	12	2
(l)	4	1	0	0	1	2	0	0	0	1	0	0	5	4
(m)	0	0	3	0	0	0	4	0	3	0	7	0	17	0
(n)	0	0	0	0	0	0	1	0	1	0	2	0	4	0
(o)	1	0	4	0	3	0	2	0	2	0	3	0	15	0
(p)	4	0	3	1	6	0	2	0	0	0	1	0	16	1
(q)	0	0	0	0	0	0	1	0	0	0	1	0	2	0
(r)	0	0	2	0	0	0	4	1	0	0	0	0	6	1
(s)	0	0	0	0	0	0	0	3	0	0	0	0	0	3
(t)	0	0	0	0	0	0	0	0	0	2	0	1	0	3
(u)	0	0	0	0	0	0	0	0	0	2	0	0	0	2
(v)	0	0	0	0	0	0	0	1	0	0	0	1	0	2
(w)	0	0	0	0	0	0	0	1	0	0	0	0	0	1
(x)	0	0	0	0	0	0	0	2	0	0	0	0	0	2
Totals	27	12	15	4	13	11	23	11	6	5	16	3	100	46

Notes: M = males   F = females

pupils considered that sex bias in textbooks had any direct effect on their mathematical competence. However, it does not follow that such bias does not affect attainment. For example, David illustrates how images in textbooks and elsewhere fed a belief system about the appropriate activities and school subjects for the two sexes:

David   In CDT and PE boys get more attention because they're doing something like football or rugby but with childcare or typing or home economics girls get more attention 'cause it's their kind of subject.

JA   Why do you say it's their sort of subject?

David   Because women do the cooking, it's a girl's subject whereas with CDT you don't see women working in a factory at technology you see a man. So it's a boy's subject or a man's subject. You don't have a woman CDT teacher you have a man and you don't have a man teacher for cooking you have a woman.

Apparently, how the subject is gendered may contribute to a sexist belief system that may have ramifications for gender relations in the school even if it does not directly affect the pupil's ability to achieve in the subject. Insofar as this belief system persuades girls that mathematics is an inappropriate subject for them they are likely to give it low priority.

English

Although English was well insulated from mathematics and French it had an open relationship with many other subjects such as geography, history, humanities and sociology. I found that historical issues (via Julius Caesar), sexism (via adverts and composition) and environmental and geographical issues (via Chernobyl and nuclear power) were explored in English lessons. Unlike mathematics classes, there was no single textbook. Teachers used a wide variety of teaching materials and the pupils' work was organized into the following themes in all sets:

Language Work

Comprehension

Factual Writing (Information)

Factual Writing (Opinion and Argument)

Imaginative Writing (Narrative)

Imaginative Writing (Description)

Aural Comprehensions

Oral Work

Literature Work

Prose Work

Play

Poetry

Projects/Extended

   Writing

I analysed five of the English textbooks used. *Julius Caesar, Great Expectations* and *Under Milk Wood* used by E1, *Hobson's Choice* used by E3, and *The Winslow Boy* used by E5. The books themselves were not defined in terms of a packaged continuum of standards like the mathematics textbooks, but teacher differentiation created stratification of school English in other ways. For example, Mr Steel (teacher of E5) once said to me:

> Try giving *Great Expectations* to my lot (E5 pupils) and see what happens.

The bottom-set pupils were not given access to this play because of teachers' expectations about how they might respond as compared with E1 pupils. Like mathematics, stratification was related to examination status. Pupils in E3 were given a sheet reading:

> During the Spring and Summer terms in the fourth year, you will need to complete enough work to fill in all the spaces on this

record sheet. This is the minimum amount of work you need to give yourself a good foundation for your work in the fifth year. If you take CSE all this work will be needed for your coursework file as evidence that you worked well in the fourth year. If you hope to take 'O' level you still need to show that you can do the work required in the fourth year to a very high standard. Your teacher will help you decide what is of good enough quality for you to include as a completed task.

I asked Ms McGuinness (teacher of E3) how she decided on the grade of a piece of work (and hence whether or not it was of high standard) apart from obvious things like grammar. She told me that 'you soon get to know what's required, what's good and what's not so good'. In other words the teacher learned the demands of the examination system and then measured the pupils' work according to that system's criteria. That measure (called 'ability') was, in turn, matched against the requirements of the system and teachers made available to pupils the kind of English work that was appropriate to the matched requirements.

Discussions about sexism could themselves form part of English teaching, but this too was affected by stratification. Ms McGuinness was prepared to discuss sex stereotyping directly with her class but she would 'also take account of the ability of the group involved on whether it merits discussion'. If she thought the group was of 'too low ability' then she would not consider it appropriate to discuss issues of sexism with the pupils. Yet if we are to believe the evidence presented by Willis (1977) a significant number of sexist boys are likely to be found in the lowest streams and these may be the most in need of anti-sexist education. However, Mr Clay (teacher of E1) admitted that he was aware that potentially sexist reading materials were sometimes given to the boys of 'low ability' in order to stimulate their interest in the subject.

Unlike mathematics lessons group work was encouraged in all the English sets. However, in E1 and E3 much more attention was paid to reading plays aloud in class than in E5. In E1, particularly, group work for preparation of project work was done in groups and the pupils were left to organize themselves and carry on the projects individually in their own time. In E5 extensive group work was practised in the classroom and supervised by the teacher. Consequently, much of the lesson time in which E1 pupils were reading and discussing the characters in plays, E5 pupils were working in groups to make a tape recording of their opinion on some topic or discussing the plan of a hypothetical bypass through an imaginary town.

This stratification is partly related to the teachers' expectations of how much homework the respective sets did. Mr Clay told me: 'It's [E1] a top set so I just let them get on with it in things like project work.' I analysed samples of the pupils' English work from E1, E3 and E5 and found that for open-ended work such as essays or opinions E1 pupils consistently wrote up to 4 or 5 pages, E3 pupils wrote about 2–3 pages and E5 pupils only about half or three-quarters of a page. E1 were often set creative writing such as essays on imagining to be a character in a play whilst E3 were more inclined to be set work related to everyday practical concerns, such as opinions of the world cup. Clearly there was knowledge differentiation related to the setting of the pupils.

My argument is *not* that this was bad teaching nor that no real 'ability' differences existed. One view of this knowledge differentiation is that some kinds of knowledge are really more appropriate for some pupils than others. According to this view knowledge differentiation is merely the playing out of real differences in 'ability' in the arena of school knowledge. However, my research suggests that the qualitative and quantitative differences between the pupils' English work does not give us an indicator of an 'ability' common to the three sets, which can account for their ranking. Certainly there are differences in the amount of effort given to open-ended work but if 'ability' is defined solely in terms of pupil effort then there is no justification for accepting that pupils in the lower sets are only capable of certain work and that those in the top set are capable of a great deal more work. To do so reinforces rather than reduces any pre-existing differences in effort between the two sets of pupils.

The teachers' view was that 'ability' in English depended a great deal on home background, or to be more precise, how much the pupils were encouraged to read by parents. This view is dependent on the assumption that the school establishment can act as a value-free independent arbiter of what counts as 'ability' in English. However, given the previous socio-logical and linguistic research on the culture clash between working-class pupils and the middle-class school (Bourdieu, 1973; Jackson and Marsden, 1962; Labov, 1972) this is a highly questionable assumption, especially since nearly all the pupils in the top sets were middle-class and nearly all the pupils in the lower sets were working-class.

The linguistic demands of the school are what the Bullock Report (1975) called 'standard English'. Yet 'standard English' is much closer to the language used by the upper middle and middle classes than that used by the working classes. Thus working-class pupils are at a considerable learning disadvantage if the educational goal is defined to be the mastery of 'standard English'. Indeed, Labov (1972) suggests that failure in reading by working-class pupils does not represent a rejection of literacy but rather a rejection of the school culture in which reading takes on a major and symbolic role. The crux is whether the speakers of 'low-status' dialects are judged by the school establishment to be linguistically *different* or linguistically *deficient*. To say that these are differences rather than deficiencies is not, of course, to deny the social power gained by speakers of 'standard English', but it does undermine the individualistic 'ability' paradigm. The English teachers in this study did not seem concerned to legitimize working-class dialects in the face of the dominant 'standard English' approach. Stratification could remain intact by maintaining the belief that there was an independent standard of English according to which some pupils were more able than others.

A greater variety of teaching materials and methods were used by the English teachers and hence the gendering of school English could occur in a much wider range of contexts than in mathematics. For this reason and because of the nature of the teaching materials used, I felt that it was inappropriate to study the gendering of school English by employing textual analysis of the kind completed for mathematics textbooks. With English texts the holistic messages were much more important.

Julius Caesar was a drama about power struggles between men and was clearly male-dominated with females being referred to as wives of male characters. None of the others could be said to be male-dominated but *Great Expectations* was concerned with the development and reflections of a boy and *The Winslow Boy* revolved around the plight of a male naval cadet. Also in *The Winslow Boy* serious jobs such as lawyer or solicitor were held by men and the only professional female character was cast as a journalist with little interest in the serious matters of reporting. On the other hand, the cause of Women's Suffrage was sometimes advocated through the central female character, Catherine. Nevertheless, fairly rigid traditional sex roles were conveyed. Whilst there was concern over the future careers of the two Winslow boys, Catherine's future was seen to be sealed once she was married.

In *Under Milk Wood* traditional sex roles were much more implicit, but two important trends in the play were significant. First, many of the female characters tended to be the wives of male characters with occupations (e.g., Butcher Benyan and Mrs Benyan). Furthermore, the female characters who had male partners were usually introduced to the audience after the males, thus emphasizing the impression that the females are merely appendages to the males. And secondly, sometimes women tended to be described as sexual objects (Thomas, 1954, pp. 48–9) and men's relationships to women solely in terms of lust (Thomas, 1954, p. 54). It was exceptional for these tendencies to occur with the sex roles reversed.

Finally, *Hobson's Choice* represented a challenge of wills between a domineering father and his eldest daughter, Maggie, who successfully opposed his authority. Maggie was the central character and she was also the most assertive especially by comparison with some of the men. In this sense traditional sex roles were reversed in the play, but it was significant that this play was a comedy and that some of the reversal of sex roles was intended to generate humour.

Several girls in E1 and E3 pointed out to me that *Julius Caesar* was male-dominated. Interestingly one boy in E3 commented that most of the parts in *Hobson's Choice* were for women. This was not actually true. There were six parts for men (two major) and five parts for women (three major) plus a part for a doctor which was defined to be male by the text. The boy seemed to be reacting to the fact that the play was *not* male-dominated. So unusual was this that it appeared to him to be female-dominated.

I found that gendering of English also occurred significantly in discussions and project work. This may be a more important socializing influence on the pupils. For example, during one classroom activity in E5 the teacher was trying to organize the pupils into groups to discuss the hypothetical planning of a bypass through a neighbourhood. He began by telling the class that they needed to choose a chair*man*. He then corrected himself and said to the class: 'I shouldn't even say chairman should I, what should I say? — chairperson'. Although the pupils were stimulated by this activity it was clearly sex-stereotyped. The pupils were told to divide themselves into several committees — the names of which were jointly agreed to be tradesmen, environmentalists, mothers and planners. Not surprisingly all the 'trades*men*' were boys, all the 'mothers' were girls and as it happened all the 'environmentalists' were girls. The 'planners' group consisted of three boys and two girls. The requirement for a 'mothers' committee' (not a parents' committee) came up in the context of who would be worried about the safety of the children. Fathers were not discussed and nor was the possibility that traders could be women. Implicit in this setting up of the problem was the idea that fathers do not worry about the safety of their children because mothers do that job! The chairperson (who was acting as an officer of the Department of the Environment) was continually referred to as 'he' by teacher and pupils. In trying to decide who to choose, the teacher asked the class what sort of qualities this officer should have. The following discussion arose:

Nigel	Might listen more to women . . . Might be more emotional.
Paul	Women are more emotional. He might be sexist.
Mr Steel	He might need to listen to arguments not emotions. He might need to be tough. Why might he be sexist Paul?
Paul	Because he's a woman's man.
Mr Steel	What, because he likes the look of them?
Paul	Yeah.

A whole range of assumptions about the roles of men and women arose from this project. On the whole, the teacher accepted rather than challenged the stereotype that women are 'emotional' and by implication not as able to be argumentative though the idea that a male chairperson should not be sexist was established. The possibility that the chairperson might be a woman was not, however, even considered.

The forming of a 'mothers' committee' seemed to be partly a result of the teacher's desire to simulate a real-life situation because most mothers are, in fact, the primary child-carers. However, the problem with this approach is that school knowledge becomes gendered in a way which reproduces, rather than debates, sex roles. Having said this, some of the girls told me later that they had enjoyed the project. In this motivational sense it was 'good' teaching. I have already mentioned that one English teacher was aware that he and other English teachers were sometimes inclined to use sexist materials to motivate boys in the bottom sets. Riddell (1992) has also reported that some male teachers in the comprehensives she studied used derogatory jokes about women to maintain boys' interest in schoolwork. This example from my observations of E5 alerts us to the point that schoolwork which is enjoyable for girls does not necessarily coincide with the challenging of patriarchal relations. Thus, the gendering of classroom discourse is not simply a matter of a sexist male conspiracy. It is rather that insufficient and unsystematic attention is given to challenging sexist assumptions.

French

Like mathematics, French was defined to be a cumulative subject. Pupils learned certain foundations on which to build further understanding. Although my observations suggested that French lessons involved a greater variety of teaching materials than mathematics they were significantly structured around the textbooks — much more so than in English.

As with mathematics there were different textbooks for the top and middle sets and these defined which knowledge systems were made available and at what pace. Framing was fairly strong but not as strong as in mathematics. The top set used *Longman Audio Visual French Stage A3* and *A4* (A3 and A4) as its main textbooks; the middle set *Longman Audio Visual French Stage B3* and *B4* (B3 and B4). The books were explicitly stratified according to the examination system. The authors of A3 stated:

> Stage A3 follows Stage A1 and A2 and is the first of three stages covering two or three years' work to 'O' level standard. For those pupils who will be likely to take CSE or no public examination the alternative version of B3 is recommended. This follows the same general material at slower pace.

The authors of B3 advised pupils studying for 'O' level to use A3. As with mathematics there was no doubt that CSE French was considered low status compared with 'O' level. This was substantiated by the fact that the top set (the 'O' level group) took a CSE paper as their end of the fourth-year exam (that is, after studying only one year of their two year 'O' level course). The teacher, Mr Sexton, told his top set pupils:

it is a compliment to you that we can feel confident about your
ability to answer these questions at this stage. It does not mean
that you have been put down for CSE in the final examinations.

This served to remind the top set that they were 'more able' than those
who *were* 'put down' for CSE and of the lower status of CSE French.

Pupils were allowed to sit where they wanted in both French sets and
the individual learning philosophy was not as prevalent as in mathematics,
but group work was rare by comparison with English. The top set used
articles from magazines and worked in groups to construct stories from
pictures whilst the middle set used another textbook specializing on the
topics of 'never', 'not', 'nothing' and 'no more' within a rather limited
vocabulary. Despite this stratification I didn't find any significant desires
to change sets on account of the subject.

Since the textbooks were so central to the structuring of the French
lessons, I decided to carry out a textual analysis of their gendering. In this
case, however, I judged that the illustrations were more likely to carry
gendering messages than a simple analysis of the occurrence of the 'masculine' and 'feminine' in the written text. As with English, the holistic
message of the story (as told by the pictures and accounts of them) was
most important. A cursory study of A3 and A4 revealed that they had
almost identical characters and style to B3 and B4. For this reason I analysed B3 and B4 and also the text entitled *The Never Not Nothing No More
Book* (NNN) used by F2, but not A3 and A4.

I found that the French textbooks were male-dominated and sex-
stereotyped. The females tended to be cooking, modelling clothes, pick-
ing flowers, waitressing, getting more pretty, shopping, fortune telling or
air hostessing. The males were gamekeepers, hunters, waiters, doctors,
tramps, police officers, customs officers, astronauts, schoolteachers, ca-
noeists, interviewers, smugglers, chauffeurs, musclebuilders, fire officers
and so on (Tables 27 and 28).

Whilst readers were told about the prettiness of young female characters no mention was made of the handsomeness of young male characters. Whilst women were shown modelling, the text discussed the skills
of the fashion designers (four men and one woman). The main difference
between these images and the male bias in the mathematics textbooks was
that female-dominated activities, which were sometimes associated with
French qualifications, such as air hostessing, modelling and secretarial work
were shown in a positive light whereas there was no evidence to suggest
that being a female mathematician had positive attractions in the mathematics textbooks. The French textbooks, then, presented a male-dominated
picture couched in gender relations which can offer positive attractions to
girls. These positive attractions were consistent with certain ways in which
the subject was perceived to be feminine in general.

Table 28: *Crude quantitative analysis of French textbooks*

Textbook	Class	Males	Females
B3	F2	155	90
B4	F2	32	22
NNN	F2	50	22
Totals		237	134

Conclusion

The stratification of school knowledge reveals most graphically how streaming reinforces the naturalization of 'ability'. The reality, however, is that pupils at different positions within the streaming hierarchy are given different workloads and targetted for different levels of examination success. Pupils in the top sets are entrusted with more extensive and challenging tasks than the other pupils, and told that they are more able than their peers in the lower sets. This knowledge differentiation occurs in the context of subcultural polarization (Chapter 4) which ironically generates support for the stratification of knowledge because the pro-school pupils expend more effort on academic work and are found mainly in the higher sets, whereas the anti-school pupils are less willing to complete school tasks and are found mainly in the lower sets. Furthermore, because of the correlation between streaming and social class the stratification of school knowledge identified in this chapter has a social-class basis.

The stratification of school knowledge and the associated naturalization of 'ability' are directly related to the issue of anti-sexist pedagogy because some teachers believe that 'lower-ability' pupils are unable to discuss and, therefore, learn about sexism. This is important because a crucial conclusion that may be drawn from the sexist gendering of texts and discourse in Greenfield is that teachers need to develop a strategy for conscious anti-sexist interventions in the classroom if they are to challenge sexism in the pedagogical process. The possibility of such interventions depends on many factors such as curriculum development, assessment procedures and the external human and economic pressures put on the school system itself. However, the convictions and commitments of teachers will also be crucial and it is to this that I turn in the next chapter.

Chapter 8

Teacher Ideology and Sex Roles in Curriculum Texts

It is common for organizational studies of schools to provide an analysis of the staff in terms of social class, qualifications, career structure and sex, but it is rare for them to concentrate on the staff's 'gender profiles'. Yet this is surely an important dimension of gendering and sexism in the process of schooling. Reducing the sexism in future publications of school texts will involve changes in the guidelines on sexism for curriculum developers and publishers. However, it will also depend centrally on changing the attitudes of teachers to such an extent that sexist materials already published do not remain in use in the classroom and so that the teacher audience to which curriculum developers and publishers address themselves is one which demands non-sexist texts and curriculum materials.

It follows that it is important to understand how teachers themselves perceive the issue of sexism in curriculum materials, especially in relation to the materials they use and their overall teaching situation. As I mentioned in Chapter 7 it is surprising that many of the research studies mentioned in this area have made no attempt to do this. School texts tend to have been analysed in a way which is abstracted from the teacher's perspectives on their use. As Kessler *et al.* (1985) have noted, discussions of sexism in education have tended to neglect teachers' aspirations and ideas about what they are doing. On the other hand, some feminist writers such as Marshall (1983) and Kenway *et al.* (1994) have considered the position of teachers developing anti-sexist initiatives. For the success of such initiatives Marshall comments on the importance of cross-school teacher support groups and Kenway *et al.* stress the need to make feminist ideas attractive and pleasurable for girls. Yet this approach to teacher perspectives on sexism in teaching materials is limited because it provides little insight into the teacher belief-systems which are likely to oppose and resist certain types of anti-sexist initiatives.

Sociological research which has focused on teacher perspectives has concentrated on such topics as the professionalization and socialization of teachers (Lortie, 1975; Lacey, 1977; Petty and Hogben, 1980; Denscombe, 1982). One common feature of this work is that the whole issue of sexism in education tends to be neglected[1] or studied only superficially (Acker, 1983, pp. 124–27). One study which stands out as an attempt to analyse teachers' perceptions of sex roles and sexism in schooling and wider society is the Australian work of Evans (1982), though his research did not lead him to any consideration of teaching materials or teachers' views of them.

In this chapter I investigate the relationships between: teachers' ideology about sex roles/sexism generally; teachers' views about sexism in curriculum materials generally; and the sexism in the curriculum materials actually used by those teachers (summarized in Chapter 7). To guide my investigation I formulated the following four basic aims in studying the teachers:

1 To construct a phenomenological account of the ideological frameworks of the teachers studied, where these frameworks are directed specifically towards issues concerning sex roles and sexism in society.
2 To explore how these ideological frameworks affect the teachers' views on sexism in curriculum texts.
3 To explore whether or not the subject specialism of secondary-school teachers is a significant intervening factor in the teachers' views on sexism in curriculum materials.
4 To test the simple hypothesis that there is a positive relationship between the teachers' general ideological frameworks and their views on sexism in their own curriculum materials. Although this hypothesis is simple it is not trivial. Keddie (1971), for example, has shown that in the case of teacher differentiation of school knowledge there can be a disparity between the apparent ideological ('educationist') framework of the teachers and situations which pertain to more specific and practical teaching tasks.

Evans (1982) carried out his research in a primary school (where the same teacher worked with the same pupils throughout the school day) because he wanted to relate teacher perceptions of sex roles solely to teacher–pupil interaction. Thus, the research here can be seen as a complementary extension of the primary-school focus of previous research into the area. In the secondary school, however, it is necessary to pay attention to ways in which subject specialisms might affect the different arguments drawn upon by teachers when considering the issue of sexism in school texts. English, mathematics and French are good subject specialisms to research from this point of view because they were well insulated from each other making the identification of perspectives based on different specialisms much easier.

Teachers were interviewed in depth using semi-structured interview techniques, usually for about two hours. All the teachers were asked two main 'lead-in' questions. Firstly, if they thought there had been any changes in sex roles in society over the previous decade. Then later in the interview they were asked whether they gave consideration to how males and females were represented in texts when selecting their curriculum materials and, if so, in what way. But before discussing the teachers' gender profiles I want to clarify how I use the term 'ideology' in this study.

'Ideology': Toward a Working Definition

Several educationalists have concentrated on 'ideology' in their writings. Usually they have been primarily concerned with the 'ideology' of/in the curriculum (Apple, 1979; Giroux, 1983b; Wexler, 1982). Unfortunately, as Dale (1986) has shown, writings on the relationship between education and 'ideology' have suffered from a lack of definitional clarity and consistency. As a solution to this problem Dale has suggested that writers should use the concept of 'ideology' to refer solely to 'those beliefs and ideas that (1) are false; (2) contribute to the reproduction of production relations and class domination; and (3) are determined and explained by the production relations' (Dale, 1986, p. 257).

My own view is that this is a much too limited definition of ideology. According to Dale's definition, ideology is irrelevant to many issues relating to sexism and racism in education (especially with respect to parts 2 and 3 of his definition). Possibly a better solution to the problems of lack of clarity in the usage of ideology is for writers to state clearly what is meant by the term in the context of their own research. My working definition of ideology is that it is a belief system which can accommodate contradictory ideas. Within an ideology there might be true and false beliefs which are systematically related and contradictory, but remain isolated and fragmented within the ideology. Consequently, the contradictions remain unresolved until challenged in some way.

Teachers' General Ideological Frameworks

Mr Bird and Ms McGuinness thought that significant changes in sex roles had taken place between the previous ten and twenty years but the other teachers interviewed thought that these changes had taken place in the previous decade. Typically the teachers mentioned the media, Greenham Common, The Women's Movement, and increased employment opportunities for women in male-dominated areas of work, as having brought issues of sexism and sex-role changes to their attention.

The teachers' explicit views of these perceived changes in sex roles fell into three categories. Ms Frost, Ms McGuinness, Mr Clay, Mr Steel and Mr Sexton were at least fairly supportive of the changes although not necessarily feminism. For example:

JA	What sort of changes [in sex roles] come to mind?
Ms McGuinness	More opportunities for women. Women play a more dominant role in society [than twenty years ago]. There aren't the assumptions about women's roles that there used to be . . .
JA	Do you welcome these changes?
Ms McGuinness	Oh yes, naturally.
JA	Why yes and why naturally?
Ms McGuinness	I'm all in favour of women having as much independence as possible. I'm against traditional sex stereotyping. Having reached the age I am and not being married or anything I naturally want to fight for what I'm doing as right. Also having seen it in my family where the girls' interests were subdued.
And: Mr Steel	Over the last decade the whole question of sex roles is under discussion in media such as the *Guardian* page for women. Media aims at this interest now. In terms of what is written nearly anything written by a woman on feminism is published even though it is pretty awful, some of it.
JA	Do you welcome these changes?
Mr Steel	Yes, definitely. Historically, there's been an assumption that the woman's role is predetermined. I come from a traditional Welsh family. My mother has never worked and I feel that her whole life has been lived within, dominated and controlled by, the family. I think other parts of her personality haven't developed.

Mr Bird and Mr Pebble opposed demands to subvert traditional sex roles. Mr Pebble was the only teacher to state, as a matter of principle, that married women with children should stay at home and look after them. His reasoning for this was that it would leave more jobs for men. This teacher also explicitly stated that he wanted to retain certain traditional sex roles such as men holding doors open for women and women not drinking pints when they go out to the pub. Mr Bird, on the other hand, quickly related the issue of sex roles to his views about The Women's Movement as a whole:

I don't approve of women's lib. I don't approve of an organization which needs to say I am a woman. I find women's lib more amusing than to be taken seriously. Peace camps at Greenham Common epitomize my hate of that type of organization.

Later in the interview Mr Bird told me that it was now more acceptable for women to take higher positions in the teaching profession. When I asked him if he welcomed this he commented: 'It's like women car drivers, they're either very good or bloody awful.' When I asked Mr Bird directly if he welcomed changes away from traditional sex roles he claimed not to care about the issue. However, I took his comments about The Women's Movement and female teachers in high positions to indicate that he was in fact opposed to such changes to some degree. Certainly he never stated any support for such changes. By contrast, Mr Counter (the third category) did seem to be genuinely nonchalant about the whole issue. He told me that he did not particularly care about changes in sex roles and that he was neither opposed to, nor threatened by, it.

During the course of the discussion about sex roles in society the topic of 'family' was raised by the teachers. However, an important sex difference emerged. The two female teachers related how traditional views of the family had given rise to personal injustices that they felt. For example, Ms Frost recalled that at an interview she had been asked if she intended to have a family. She felt sure that the interviewers asked the question on the assumption that because she was a woman she would be taking time out of the profession to look after children. On the other hand, the male teachers tended to relate their lifestyle to those of their parents in a way which demonstrated how they were less traditional than their parents.

For Mr Sexton and Mr Steel (both married with children) and Mr Clay who was living with a female partner and contemplating having a first child, the issue of childcare was a common theme in considering the challenges they made to traditional sex roles in their lifestyles. Although all these teachers acknowledged their responsibility for looking after their own children none had considered the possibility that they would give up their job to do the childcare full-time. In all cases this possibility had been considered for the women partners involved. Even Mr Bird (also married with children) was keen to mention his contribution to home duties.

| JA | Did you consider that *you* would give up your job to look after the children? |
| **Mr Bird** | No, that was never considered, but we did consider getting an *au pair* girl or farming them [his children] out to grandmother . . . We would share cleaning. I stay with my son on Saturday morning whilst she is shopping. I have a baby-sitting role and do washing up, laundry and Sunday-lunch cooking. |

The family and home duties were fruitful topics for discussion in the interviews. These topics were part of what I refer to as the teachers' 'domain of acceptable discourse about gender relations.' So male childcaring was included in the acceptable discourse although, as Mr Steel reveals, how far may be limited:

> I'll tell you *but don't tell anyone else for God's sake.* My wife works. On Friday the kids were on holiday. We are not assuming that she has to take the day off so I'm taking the day off. It's only a small thing but how many deputy heads would do it? (my emphasis)

However, all the teachers distanced themselves from confronting the substance of feminist arguments or feminist political philosophies. I am not suggesting that this was a conscious ploy but rather that the teachers' ideological frameworks 'policed' the boundaries between acceptable and unacceptable discourses. There were two central features of these ideological frameworks. Feminist arguments tended to be substituted by 'popular' stereotypes/images of feminism. In some cases the whole of feminism was then judged on the basis of an evaluation of these stereotypes. Second, for the teachers opposed to changes in traditional sex roles, feminism tended to be dismissed on the grounds that women could be found who disagreed with it or that women's liberation had already been achieved. The following three examples illustrate these points.

JA	Would you describe yourself as a feminist?
Ms McGuinness	Probably, mmm, I don't know, not a radical feminist. The word implies chaining yourself to Greenham Common. I'm more conservative. Some of the extremes they go to do nothing for the cause of women. Obviously, you stand up for your own sex.
JA	What do you think about feminism?
Mr Pebble	It doesn't do the cause of women much good. Even women tend to despise the way active feminists go about their convictions. People are sick and tired of it.
Mr Bird	You talk about the women's peace camp — it's a sexist thing because it has been created as sexist. The women's libbers, of whom, there are a few in the school as teachers and pupils give an unbalanced point of view. They're fighting for something they've got and already got it. I don't think that's just a male comment, other women staff have made similar comments.

Table 29: Teachers' views on sex–stereotyping in curriculum materials

Pro- to anti-feminist ideology	Most to least challenging to sexist texts
(top to bottom)	(top to bottom)
Ms McG	Ms McG
Ms Fr	Ms Fr
Mr Cl	Mr Co
Mr St	Mr Cl (tie)
Mr Se	Mr St (tie)
Mr Co	Mr Se
Mr Bi	Mr Bi
Mr Pe	Mr Pe

On the basis of the interview data concerning the teachers' views on sex roles, the family and feminism, it was possible to rank the teachers' ideologies along an axis running from anti-traditional sex roles/pro-feminist to pro-traditional sex roles/anti-feminist yielding the above result (Table 29).

Teachers' Views on Sex-stereotyping in Curriculum Materials

Three of the teachers, Mr Pebble, Mr Bird and Mr Sexton, thought that the issue of sex-stereotyping in curriculum materials was not important. Mr Pebble reiterated several times that in selecting his curriculum materials he did not consider how males and females were represented in the text. This viewpoint was further reinforced when he commented:

> The only thing I have to worry about is that grammatically when girls write they must distinguish between girls' and boys' endings.

He was the only teacher to explicitly state that he thought the issue was not only unimportant in his own subject (French) but in any subject.

Mr Bird saw the issue as trivial for mathematics teaching. However, unlike Mr Pebble, he had clearly given the issue some thought and admitted to having felt irritated in the past for having to think about it. Nevertheless, he seemed to be somewhat inconsistent about whether he thought mathematics textbooks actually had a male bias.

Mr Bird   The idea that is being put forward that if you have a boy in the first question you must have a girl in the second question irritates you. It doesn't occur to you. It irritated me when it was first mooted a few years ago. It's like some of these strange groups in London education authorities which say that if you have a picture of a black person then you should take note. Suddenly people started saying make sure it's got equal representation. If you actually analyse maths textbooks you will find they are male-dominated.

JA Are you glad this was pointed out to you?

Mr Bird No, not particularly.

JA Do you resent that it's been pointed out to you?

Mr Bird I made a joke of it I suppose. In writing an exam paper you now find that just so as not to offend anyone you ought to swap things around a little bit rather than putting people into categories. It takes longer when you have to think about this in the back of your mind. I don't think it's important in maths . . . On the whole maths material tended to be non-sexist material anyway. I don't think a boys' or girls' maths book exists. See this debate on sex typing in maths textbooks is trivial. I can't think of one which is unbalanced in the sense of being geared towards boys or girls.

Mr Bird did indeed make a joke of the issue even in class as Kate explains, but for Kate this made the implicit sexism worse.

JA What about maths? Do you notice that the questions are mostly about boys' or girls' activities?

Kate Well, the teacher [Mr Bird] is very aware of this. Sometimes he'll write up a question with 'men' in it and then stroke it out and put 'people' because some girls might get irate about it. But the teacher takes the mickey out of the girls and this makes it worse because the boys want a fuss to be made so that they can make further comments about it.

Mr Sexton did admit that French texts had been very sex-stereotyped in the past but thought that this situation no longer persisted. Although he welcomed these changes he did not consider that it was a serious issue because he was 'more interested in the content from a language point of view'.

Unlike Mr Bird, Ms Frost and Mr Counter were quite definite that mathematics textbooks were biased in favour of boys by being male-dominated and emphasizing male-dominated activities.

Mr Counter Quite a lot of the examples in the textbook will be male-dominated and even when the example could be either sex; but the females tend to be put in the textbook in traditional female roles. Our textbook

tends to be very male. Males also tend to be better
represented in what they do. Even with some of
the new textbooks we have, there doesn't seem
to be much of a swap of sex roles. Possibly the
older generation men don't even think about it.
In the class pupils have already mentioned the
male-dominated examples on several occasions. It's
always the girls who mentioned it, never the boys.
Basically, some of the girls would be quite happy
to do something for women's lib but for others it
didn't seem to matter.

Ms Frost and Mr Counter were both clearly aware of the issue and,
as I witnessed in classroom observation, they did design some examples
which involved girls more than the textbook examples. These two teachers
also felt that the more modern textbooks were at most only marginally
less male-dominated. However, Ms Frost had made the effort to break
away from the rather dated *Simple Modern Maths* series. She felt that male
domination in mathematics textbooks was particularly important to counter because some of the girls in her class had already told her that mathematics was a boy's subject. However, her strategy for dealing with this
issue was based on the shaky assumption that girls necessarily have less
interest in substantive mathematical problems.

Ms Frost   If you're teaching girls they will be more concerned
with the appearance of the topic whereas with the boys
— they are more inclined to ask where am I going to
use this when I leave school? Girls tend to be more
interested just by appearance . . . Some of the workcard
systems where there are a lot of geometrical patterns
and so on say 'colour this in' it is designed to appeal
more to the girls but, on the other hand, they take
more time on this whereas the boys are not likely to
want to do this. And so this appeases girls rather than
increasing their understanding.

Of the three English teachers, only Ms McGuinness was clearly committed to selecting curriculum materials with a view to debating and
challenging traditional sex roles. She complained that in Dickens' works
women tended to be characterized as submissive and feminine and said
that she would confront the class with such issues in the course of her
teaching. In the classes I observed she had also got the class to debate and
write their opinions about the representation of women in a sexist news-
paper advert. She had also chosen *Hobson's Choice* as E3's class play because it inverted traditional sex roles and, therefore, provided a context to

discuss sex-stereotyping and the general representations of men and women in texts. Mr Clay and Mr Steel were aware of the issue of sex-stereotyping in curriculum materials and, in fact, referred me to several texts for English classes which tried to tackle the issue from a progressive (i.e., anti-traditional sex roles) viewpoint. However, these two teachers did not use such texts in their own teaching, claiming that they had not yet thought about how to incorporate these progressive approaches into their own classes.

Using interview data and some observational data I ranked the teachers' views on texts and selection of curriculum materials on a scale ranging from most challenging of traditional sex roles in texts to least challenging (Table 29).

Table 29 shows the relationship between the teachers' ideological frameworks and their views on curriculum materials. A positive relationship is clearly evident and at the 'extremes' of the rankings there is a perfect fit. Thus the data support the hypothesis that teachers' ideological perspectives on sex roles strongly influences their attitude towards designing, and/or introducing in the classroom, non-sexist or anti-sexist curriculum materials.

Regarding the curricular texts used, only Ms McGuinness was successful in building into her teaching an element of anti-sexist content. This further substantiates the claim that teacher ideology significantly influences teachers' selection of texts with respect to sex roles.

Conclusion

Before drawing out some of the conclusions from this chapter some of the other variables involved are worth some consideration. The data are suggestive that the sex of the teacher influenced his or her ideological framework (the two teachers holding the most anti-traditional sex roles were women and they both related this anti-traditionalism to personal injustices at the hands of sexism). However, the age of the teacher did not seem to be associated with any particular general ideological perspectives (despite Mr Counter's suggestion that age might be a major factor) and nor did it seem to affect teachers' views on sexism in curriculum materials in a way that was independent of their general ideologies. The evidence also suggests that streaming did not have a significant impact on the extent of sexist curriculum materials use, e.g., the top streams did not receive significantly less sexist texts than the bottom streams or vice versa. On the other hand, Ms McGuinness and Mr Clay did comment that they *might not* raise issues of sexism with a 'low-ability' class. These comments suggest that with a group of teachers committed to anti-sexist pedagogy streaming *might* be a much more significant factor.

It could be argued that some of the teachers' responses to questions about curriculum materials were affected by their subject specialism rather than their general ideological perspectives on sex roles. For example, Mr Bird's claim that mathematics texts have been fairly non-sexist and the French teachers' view of their role as being only concerned with the content of French texts 'from a language point of view'. It could be argued that mathematics and French teachers tend to adopt 'transmission' and 'interpretation' pedagogies and, therefore, they tend to neglect the wider context of learning (Barnes, 1976, pp. 139–57). This narrow approach to learning and teachers' educational responsibilities is facilitated by the algorithmic perspective mentioned in Chapter 7.

This is a valid point and there is probably an interactive relationship between teachers' general ideologies, on the one hand, and the development of subcultural values related to subject specialism on the other. However, with respect to issues of sexism the latter does seem to be much more epiphenomenal. Mr Bird's assessment of mathematics texts as non-sexist is an indication of his limited view of what counts as being sexist and this is surely a function of his ideological framework. Similarly, the French teachers' notion that language teaching is separate from the sexist or non-sexist context in which the language is practised and learned is surely dependent on an ideology that accepts certain forms of sexist language and text. Moreover, ideological orientations in relation to sexism do not seem to be significantly influenced by subject specialism, although English was the only subject in which all the teachers in the sample supported changes in traditional sex roles.

The findings outlined in this chapter indicate that teachers' general ideology about sex roles is a major factor in determining their willingness to use non-sexist or anti-sexist curriculum materials. My research implies that even teachers who are sympathetic to the changes away from traditional sex roles will not necessarily implement a reduction in the sex stereotyping of their own curriculum materials (e.g., Mr Clay and Mr Steel). Only the teachers who feel committed to challenging traditional sex roles seem likely to implement changes in their own curriculum materials (e.g., Ms McGuinness).

On the assumption that the goal of reducing sexism in curriculum materials is a desirable one the major implication of this research is that attempts to reach that goal without taking into account teachers' more general and fundamental beliefs about sex roles and sexism are likely to experience a certain degree of failure because of teacher resistance. In this respect the future role of teacher education seems crucial. It is likely to be much easier to debate sexism in the curriculum in the context of teacher education than to attract teachers such as Mr Bird or Mr Pebble to the relevant types of in-service courses.

The nature of the anti-feminist ideology espoused by some of the teachers in this study admits no obvious mechanism of persuasion to adopt an anti-sexist stance. Nevertheless, on the basis of this study it seems that some demystification of feminism might be one effective strategy of persuasion since this could counter the adoption of images of feminism in place of feminist arguments. An important part of this demystification should entail reiterating the point that feminism is not *just* about 'women's issues', rather that it addresses issues concerning the social relations between the sexes. Another strategy might be to use elements of the acceptable discourse about sex roles to connect with broader feminist arguments which challenge sexist ideology at its roots.

Note

1 However, Lacey (1977) does give some consideration to how the career structure of the teaching profession favours men.

Chapter 9

Conclusions, Implications and Social Change

An analysis of comprehensive education should consider carefully the appropriate forms of school organization as well as the performance 'output' of schools. Comprehensive education ought to be concerned with equality and social solidarity between not only social classes but also genders. By highlighting some of the ways in which social divisions can occur within school this study suggests how gender and class divisions could be reduced.

My research implies that streaming by sets is likely to accentuate social-class differences in academic performance through polarization effects on the pupil population. Of course, such organizational antecedents of social-class differences should be regarded as augmenting such relevant cultural differences as already exist prior to, and during, pupils' secondary schooling. There is much social-class culture conflict between working-class pupils and the middle-class school which is independent of streaming as Jackson and Marsden (1962), Willis (1977; 1981), Humphries (1981) and Giroux (1983b) have noted. Nevertheless, streaming is a form of differentiation that is specifically imposed by school institutions. On the evidence adduced in this book secondary schools that wish to embrace the egalitarian and integrative ideals of comprehensive education might be well advised to avoid streaming even by sets.

Chapter 5 shows that conflicting gender-value systems can also give rise to polarization both between pupils and between teachers and pupils. Sometimes this has an impact on the extent, and nature, of anti-school behaviour that can, in turn, have an impact on academic performance. My study of Greenfield Comprehensive suggests that little progress has been made in breaking down conflicting gender-value systems of deviant boys in comprehensive schools. This may be because of the neglect of gender as an integral part of the comprehensive educational ideals.

I have also argued that resistance theory contains some definitional problems which perhaps render the label 'resistor' fairly ambiguous. Nevertheless, gauging the range of definitions contained in resistance research from Anyon's generous all-encompassing definition to the very narrow, but rigorous, definition of Aggleton and Whitty, it may be concluded that there was some resistance to the schooling system at Greenfield but, in contrast to Willis's argument, it was not upheld by the anti-school working-class 'lads' but rather by some other anti-school pupils. The 'left idealist' critique of schooling is that it is a predominantly middle-class institution attempting to change working-class culture. However, as regards 'the lads''s sexism, which by no means exhausts working-class culture, there is need for change that the school does not always pursue with sufficient vigour.

I have also considered how the organization and processing of school knowledge (via the stratification and gendering of texts) provides a setting which is not sufficiently critical of dominant social class and gender divisions to discourage their reproduction within further schooling and out into the occupational structure. In this regard it may be noted that destreaming could reduce the polarization between 'supportive' and 'non-supportive' groups and change friendship patterns so that they gave less support to conservative peer pressure about subject options. Furthermore, the curriculum needs to include time for critical debate about the relationship between subjects, sex roles, occupational status and career expectations. Careers lessons or 'advice' which give pupils 'the facts about life opportunities' are inadequate and sometimes misleading. As a first step, what is required instead of merely introducing 'progressive' options into the prevailing option system is a major decoupling of the curriculum from the dominant assumptions which determine what subjects are appropriate for certain life paths, genders and social classes. This needs to be done *in conjunction with* minimizing the crippling effects of the naturalization of abilities as reinforced by streaming into 'successes' and 'failures'.

My research indicates that it is an oversimplification to suppose that secondary schooling reproduces the wider social-class structure merely by being in 'correspondence' with it (Bowles and Gintis, 1976; Mickelson, 1980). The correspondence theory of schooling claims that within schools social class *determines* the behavioural norms of pupils and the behavioural expectations of teachers. Middle-class pupils, it is argued, are encouraged to fulfil innovative and leadership roles whilst working-class pupils are encouraged to be passive, subordinate and punctual. Leaving aside the point that many of the anti-school attitudes reported in this study do not reflect passivity, subordination or punctuality, the factor missing from the correspondence theory is the pupils' relationship to the values of the school as a social institution. That relationship is related to, but not determined by social class and gender.

The analysis of teachers' set stereotyping and the associated ability ideology in Chapter 4 illustrates how teachers' ideology can unconsciously discriminate against working-class pupils because they are mostly to be found in the lower sets. The analysis in Chapter 8 complements that analysis with respect to gender by focusing on teachers' ideology about sex roles especially in relation to the gendering of school knowledge discussed in Chapter 7. The evidence in Chapter 8 suggests that teachers' general ideology about sex roles strongly influences their specific judgments in relation to teaching and choice of curriculum materials just as the teachers' general ideology about 'ability' and sets was found to affect the teachers' specific judgments about teaching approaches independently of other factors.

My findings suggest that significant changes to the interpersonal relations of schooling in line with the integrative and egalitarian principles of comprehensive education could be achieved by implementing particular organizational changes. These are:

- further reduction in the extent of streaming by sets and possibly moving towards complete 'mixed-ability' classes with resources to meet the demands of 'mixed-ability teaching';
- a reduction in intra-set differentiation by decreasing the emphasis on a competitive individual learning philosophy and increasing cooperative curricular activities;
- reduction in sex-stereotyping of pupils by allowing the pupils to develop a broader diversity of gender identity — e.g., elimination of school uniform (essentially an inherited grammar-school phenomenon) and use of sex differences as a form of social control in the school;
- introduction of an interventionist policy by the school in relation to the subject-option process which appreciates the limitations of the ideology of free choice and tries to minimize socio-cultural reproduction of the dominant social class and gender assumptions;
- the creation of sufficient time within secondary teacher-training programmes to allow trainees to develop a good awareness of the complexities of gender and class divisions in society and education in particular;
- the development amongst the staff of a clear anti-sexist pedagogy, including a policy towards sexism in school texts, so that instances of sexism in the learning process can be tackled in a systematic and educational way;
- the development of a more reflective curriculum capable of relating pupils' experiences to issues of class and gender divisions in society with a view to reinforcing the integrative and egalitarian principles of comprehensive education.

Implementing some or all of these changes might be at the expense of the meritocratic principle. The school might not produce so many highly qualified pupils as measured by certificates. However, even on the purely meritocratic principle there would probably be the improvement that there would be fewer anti-school pupils and, therefore, fewer pupils with bad behaviour records, missed assignments and ultimately fewer pupils with very poor qualifications. Moreover, anti-school pupils are particularly demanding for teachers and the resources of the school. A reduction in the number of anti-school pupils would probably release more teaching time and resources for all the pupils, including the 'most able'. Unfortunately, the changes that have occurred within the British educational system since I conducted my fieldwork are unlikely to tackle the problems of gender and class polarization identified in this book, and may accentuate some of them.

The Empire Strikes Back

Since 1986 successive Conservative Governments have introduced a number of major changes to secondary education in England and Wales. The centre-piece of those changes was the 1988 Education Reform Act which the Government claims will increase 'parental choice' and raise 'educational standards' by making state schools more accountable to parents and employers. The Act has four basic features: open enrolment; the local management of schools (LMS); the encouragement of grant-maintained (GM) schools; and the imposition of a national curriculum with associated testing and assessment procedures (Bash and Coulby, 1989).

By open enrolment is meant that Local Education Authorities (LEAs) are now stripped of their power to determine the limits to admission for their schools. Previously LEAs had planned the size and number of schools in a particular area. This provided a balance between parental choice and the LEA's desire to avoid the wasteful and inequitous situation in which one school might be packed to full capacity while its neighbour might be two-thirds empty. Since the implementation of the Education Reform Act, LEAs are no longer permitted such planning. Rather, the physical capacity of the school is now the only valid limit on admissions to a school and the 'market' of 'parental choice' is given maximum sovereignty, at least in theory.

The introduction of LMS requires LEAs to delegate control of school budgets and the financial management of schools to governors and headteachers. LEAs are still required to finance the running of their schools based on 'aggregate schools budgets', but they no longer have any role in more detailed financial decisions. For example, it is now school governors who can decide on the numbers of teaching and non-teaching staff in their school.

Under the new legislation the Government has also encouraged schools to 'opt out' of LEA control, that is, to become GM schools. Such schools receive their funding directly from central government which finances them on the basis of what their LEAs would have provided had they not opted out. The main difference between a GM school and LMS is that in the former the amount previously retained by the LEA for property maintenance, central administration, advisory and inspection services, legal and accounting services and other support services is given directly to the school (Davies and Anderson, 1992). In effect, GM schools are self-governing and the LEAs have no role in their management. Whether a school opts out is decided by a majority in a ballot of the parents of the children at the school at the time of the ballot. Governors can decide to hold a ballot and must consider doing so every year and report their decision to parents. Moreover, parents can force governors to hold a ballot if enough parents so petition — the number of parents signing the petition must equal at least 20 per cent of the number of pupils registered at the school (Department for Education, 1994).

Prior to 1988 in secondary schools the range of subjects to be taught and the time allocated to them were mainly determined by the headteacher in consultation with staff. In particular the curriculum of secondary schools held a great deal in common and this was especially true within subjects in post-14 secondary education because teachers tended to offer curricula consistent with the demands of GCSE examination-board syllabuses. However, the Education Reform Act stipulated a curriculum to be taught and assessed in all state secondary schools throughout England and Wales. It became compulsory for pupils to study English, mathematics, science, a modern foreign language, history, geography, technology, music, art and physical education (and Welsh in Welsh-speaking areas) from the ages of 5 to 16. The subject-option process discussed in Chapter 6 was virtually abolished because almost the entire curriculum was prescribed. Moreover, attainment targets were to be established for these subjects at four key stages — generally at ages 7, 11, 14 and 16. Pupils were to be tested at these ages so that their performance could be assessed against the attainment targets. To these ends the Government established an advisory task group for each of the national curriculum subjects and a task group on assessment and testing (TGAT). Following the advice of TGAT the Government is now seeking to publish the results of national-curriculum tests in all secondary schools in the form of league tables so that parents can compare the results of different schools. In addition all state schools, primary and secondary, are required to provide parents with a prospectus each year which includes the school's test results and compares them with the local and national results (Department for Education, 1994).

The implementation of the Education Reform Act has been a near shambles. It became an enormous bureaucratic burden for teachers to accommodate such a heavily prescribed national curriculum, which together with a load of testing persuaded the vast majority of them to oppose the testing regime. In the spring and summer of 1993 96 per cent of the members of the National Union of Teachers and 88 per cent of the National Association of Schoolmasters and Union of Women Teachers voted in favour of boycotting the national-curriculum tests. Consequently, only 5 per cent of state secondary schools in England and Wales conducted the tests for 14-year-olds that year (Judd, 1993; Meikle, 1994a) and in summer 1994 less than 10 per cent of the schools implemented the national-curriculum tests for English, mathematics *and* science (Meikle, 1994c).

In response to such widespread opposition by teachers the Government has decided to slim down the subjects and the testing within the national curriculum. The Government's advisers, most notably, Sir Ron Dearing's School Curriculum and Assessment Authority, felt it necessary to cut the amount of material tested at some stages for some subjects by as much as two-thirds (Sweetman, 1994b). Most importantly for the research in this book the content of the national curriculum for ages 14 to 16 (that is, fourth and fifth years at secondary school) has now been reduced to include only English, mathematics, science, technology and a modern foreign language, and to take up no more than 60 per cent of curriculum time (Department for Education, 1994; Sweetman, 1994a). Thus, Sir Ron Dearing's final review of the national curriculum re-introduced space for post-14 subject options in 40 per cent of the curriculum. This means that researching the subject-option process, as I reported in Chapter 6, has not become socially irrelevant because of the national curriculum — a conclusion jumped to by some commentators such as Lees (1993). Nevertheless, the study of science, technology and a modern foreign language for boys and girls in the fourth and fifth years probably heralds the end of concerns about girls opting out of science at this early stage. On the other hand, compulsory science *and* technology is suggestive of an overly technocratic curriculum geared towards the promotion of the New Right's 'enterprise culture' (Elliot and MacLennan, 1994). It remains to be seen whether post-14 science and technology become popular among girls, and whether the compulsory subjects of the national curriculum will be reduced further.

Regarding the Government's efforts to persuade schools to 'opt out' of LEA control, by 3 May 1994 only 949 GM schools were operating or had been approved out of a total 24,706 eligible schools and only 1,504 ballots had been held implying that the vast majority of school governors and parents had no interest in the prospect of opting out (Anon, 1994b). In the light of these results the Government's insistence that every school governing body must consider opting out at least once a year shows a degree of contempt for democracy — a requirement to 'keep on voting until you make the right choice' (Meikle, 1994b). To add insult to injury in the summer of 1993 the Government admitted that at least 99 of the 493 opt-out schools then up and running were to have their day-to-day spending budgets for the year cut by as much as £100,000 in some cases (Meikle, 1993).

Despite the lack of enthusiasm for the Government's education reforms among schools and the teaching profession it would be a mistake to think that they have had no impact on comprehensive education. They have created a climate in which competition between schools and between parents features much more extensively than before. The open enrolment policy has increased the likelihood that popular schools will become larger or more selective in their intakes while the other less popular schools 'sink' (Elliot and MacLennan, 1994). The prospect of covert selection threatens to further erode not only the egalitarianism and integrative ideals of comprehensive education outlined in Chapter 1, but also the meritocratic principle. This point has been raised by commentators at the OECD who argue that an education system driven by parental choice can increase social-class polarization:

> There is a danger that under such a system schools will become more polarized in terms of reputation and the social class of their intake ... Any tendency to cluster may potentially work against opportunities for pupils from working-class families by concentrating socially disadvantaged children. (cited in MacLeod, 1994)

There is some evidence that polarization between popular and unpopular secondary schools has already occurred, accentuated by the publication of league tables of school examination results (Tytler, 1994).

Furthermore, in 1993 John Patten, Secretary of State for Education, announced that three GM secondary schools were to introduce entrance examinations to assist them in their selection procedures (Bennetto, 1993). This could result in the growth of a selective secondary-education system in which only pupils who reach a certain mark/grade in entrance tests are permitted to attend some schools. Such concerns are not without foundation. Preliminary research on GM schools suggests that 30 per cent of the first 100 comprehensives to gain GM status were covertly selecting using school reports, interviews or tests and in March 1994 it was reported that GM schools in Dorset, Barnet, Lambeth, Sutton and Wandsworth were aiming to become fully or partially selective by taking between 30 and 100 per cent of pupils on grounds of ability (Croall, 1994).

The LMS provisions have also fuelled a business-oriented self-interested ethic borne of insecurity among headteachers (Bates, 1990; Ward, 1991). Under LMS school governors and headteachers turn their attention fundamentally to balancing the books in their school (Beckett, 1992; Bowe, Ball and Gold, 1992, pp. 112–13). Thoughts on the nature and purposes of education beyond instrumental survival of their institution increasingly take a back seat and even teachers opposed to the Government's educational reforms may not resist them in their own institutional context (Gilborn, 1994). There are also reports that the allocation of funds to schools on the basis of the average rather than real costs of items under LMS has led to substantial inequalities in the resources made available to schools. This, combined with the anxieties of school governors and headteachers about running into deficit, has created a situation in which some schools have handsome surpluses up to £200,000, while others cut teaching staff in order to balance the books (MacLeod, 1993; Vaughan,

1990). From their research into some cases of LMS, Bowe, Ball and Gold (1992, p. 81) report:

> The picture is not one of new freedoms. Rather the new elements introduced by LMS require schools to deal with a different, expanded and contradictory set of demands. In trying to adjust to these demands schools are finding the new era . . . massively pressured and often a distraction from the world of educating students. Important issues about the purposes of schooling in our society are being thrown up by the implementation of LMS, but they are not being addressed in public debate.

Pressure on resources is leading to larger classes. Teachers have also felt the greater demands being made on them by the national curriculum. Consequently, proposals have grown not for destreaming in secondary schools, as I have suggested, but for the introduction of streaming into primary schools. Such streaming was encouraged by a Government Circular in 1989 which implied that schools could decide to stream pupils as an easier way of implementing the national curriculum and testing (Weston, 1989a). The Government suggested that the 'most able' primary children could be put up a class and take the new curriculum tests early; while in secondary schools there could be a 'fast stream' in which the 'most able' pupils could be allowed to drop some national-curriculum subjects and specialize once they had reached a particular level (Judd, 1990).

In 1991 the leader of the National Association of Head Teachers was reported as calling for streaming in the last two years of primary schools not because he thought that mixed-ability teaching had failed primary children but because of the demands of the national curriculum (Berliner, 1991). The reason for this is that mixed-ability teaching generally requires more resources and a more highly developed level of teaching skills than streaming. Thus, under current Government policies organizational differentiation is likely to become more widespread.

The Government persistently represents the Education Reform Act as legislation that has increased 'parent power' and 'parent choice' in education. In fact, the major effect of the Act has been to undermine local democracy. In a poll of 4,882 adults in inner London in 1988 71 per cent of parents with children at Inner London Education Authority (ILEA) schools were strongly opposed to the abolition of ILEA, and out of the overall sample 60 per cent were opposed while 20 per cent supported abolition (Fairhall, 1988). Yet the Government went ahead with its plans to break up ILEA under its Education Reform Act. Such undermining of LEA power is particularly significant to our concerns because some LEAs were amongst the most committed advocates of gender equality (Burton and Weiner, 1990). Furthermore, while LEAs are elected by the entire adult population in a particular area, the ballots on whether a school should opt for GM status are of the parents whose children are currently at that school. The parents of children who might want to use the school in the future have no say in the matter whatsoever. The reforms have also extended the powers of non-elected 'quangos', such as the Funding Agency for Schools which distributes money to GM schools, and enhanced the influence of unelected business interests on school governing bodies (Anon, 1994a).

The publication of league tables of schools' examination results is also supposedly part of the present Government's policy to increase parents' choices about schools. However, as Goldstein (1991) has argued, this procedure of ranking schools by using the average test scores of their pupils is likely to be misleading and unfair. Social scientific research into the 'effectiveness' or 'performance' of schools suggests that publishing raw examination results as a means for providing parents with tools to identify effective and poor schools is simply wrong (Gow, 1989). This is because aggregate examination results on a school basis do not give an accurate picture of what is happening to individual pupils within the school.

The achievements of pupils at the end of a period of schooling are strongly associated with their achievements at the beginning of that period. Hence, any sensible measurement of school effectiveness needs to be concerned with pupils' progress during their period at the school (the 'value added' by the school). This requires the analysis of individual pupils' scores while at that school, taking account of pupil achievement on entry to the school. Consequently, the Government's 'performance league tables', which cannot do this, are likely to reflect to a large extent factors such as selective intake rather than school effectiveness. Moreover, research suggests that schools cannot be sensibly ranked along a single dimension because they differ in many respects and have different effects on different kinds of children (Goldstein and Nuttall, 1989; Weston, 1990). Yet despite the inadequacies of such league tables they have diverted attention away from important debates about the social purposes of education. Increasingly schooling is being represented as a production line for certification/examination results.

Not even the Conservative Government attempts to present the introduction of a national curriculum as increasing parental choice. It might be better presented as a mechanism for ideological control. The 1988 Education Reform Act established three new bodies, the National Curriculum Council (NCC), the Curriculum Council for Wales and the Schools Examinations and Assessment Council, which were appointed by the Secretary of State to advise him about curriculum content and assessment. The Government's approach to appointing its 'expert' advisers on these matters may be ideological. According to Bash and Coulby (1989, p. 58) Prime Minister Thatcher intervened to block the appointment to the NCC of people 'whom she considered to be politically of different persuasions from herself'. Besides, the councils are merely advisory, allowing the Secretary of State for Education to accept the more agreeable portions of their advice and to reject the less palatable parts. In effect, issues concerning the detailed content of the curriculum, previously seen as matters involving professional judgment have been devolved to a layperson, the Secretary of State.

Some of the subjects most likely to encourage pupils' reflection upon gender and class divisions, such as sociology, social studies, politics and economics are conspicuous by their absence from the national curriculum. As one commentator has observed, the national curriculum may facilitate indoctrination rather than an education suited to the demise of class divisions and patriarchy:

> A most powerful way of indoctrinating pupils is by so organizing their studies that certain kinds of reflection, about political matters, for instance, are off the agenda. This was not possible for governments to achieve directly before the recent shift from professional control of curricula; but now by filling school timetables with safe subjects, determining much of the syllabuses to be covered, and by focusing teachers' attention on getting pupils through national tests, preventing thought about fundamental values is a much more feasible task. (White, 1988, pp. 121–2)

Whatever the risks of indoctrination the national curriculum certainly reflects a grammar-school tradition with its orientation towards disintegrated subjects. Emphasis has also shifted to concerns about the importance of testable standard English and the efficiency of transmission pedagogy for algorithmic mathematics as well as other subjects (Bates, 1991; Burton and Weiner, 1990; Judd and Strickland, 1993; Meikle, 1990; Weston, 1989b). This is likely to reinforce the individual learning philosophy in English and mathematics classes rather than encourage cooperative learning situations.

Government efforts at ideological control over school have also extended to transforming teacher training. Under Education Secretary Kenneth Clarke and then John Patten, the Government has sought to undermine the influence of higher-education institutions in teacher training by insisting that school-centred training should be increased (Sweetman, 1993). This measure will probably increase the emphasis on teachers' classroom-management skills and make less time available for discussing matters such as how best to develop anti-sexist initiatives in school and why an appreciation of gender and class differences among pupils is important.

These proposals have been followed by more direct and explicit ideological messages from senior Government officials. At the 1993 Conservative Party conference the Education Secretary, John Patten, brought 'traditional family values' back into the education debate. He argued that the family was fundamental to education and in a BBC interview he revealed what he regarded to be the most desirable type of family by agreeing that schools should teach that married couples are preferable to unmarried couples and heterosexual couples preferable to homosexual couples (Bellos, 1993).

Such Government pronouncements have led to undue emphasis being given to arguments that confuse the importance of caring and meaningful relationships between parents with the married heterosexual nuclear family (see Phillips, 1993). There is no guarantee that two stable parents are better than one, though often that may be the case (Bellos, 1993). Even when that is the case it is not obvious what, if anything, follows from such a finding unless it is being assumed that couples with children separate flippantly. It is even less obvious why such couples must be better parents because they are married or heterosexual.

Debates about responsible parenting and the role of parents in children's education are valuable, but it is important that they do not result in a growth of patriarchal values in education or eclipse discussions about gender differentiation in schools. These are real dangers because of the New Right's agenda on traditional morality. During the 1960s and 1970s feminists made some progress in challenging the idea that the dominant gender relations that existed were right. However, one goal of the New Right is to reassert and naturalize a set of common sense taken-for-granted views that existing patriarchal gender relations are right (Elliot and MacLennan, 1994).

Some commentators believe that the Conservative Government's educational reforms reflect an attachment to a golden era of 'Victorian values where positivism, imperialism and patriarchy abounded — and where each person knew their social place and Imperial Britain reigned supreme' (Burton and Weiner, 1990). Whatever the accuracy of this characterization, the reforms are certainly unlikely to reduce gender or class divisions in society. On the contrary, most of them offer nothing to promote anti-sexist initiatives in education, may even undermine such initiatives, and are likely to reproduce and amplify class differences, contributing to a more unequal society (Ball, 1993).

My final conclusion, therefore, is a pessimistic one as regards the prospects for comprehensive education. Since 1976 when the Labour Prime Minister Callaghan opened the Great Debate on education an opportunity to build a more egalitarian school system fostering critical citizenship, greater social solidarity between classes and more sensitivity towards gender relations and the diversity of abilities was missed. This is not surprising given the anti-egalitarian views of the New Right that has come to dominate successive Conservative Governments since 1979. Consequently, the ideals of comprehensive education continue to be compromised and policies of 'divide and school' have taken on a new momentum.

Note

1 The Scottish Education Minister, Michael Forsyth, declared that Scotland already had a national curriculum in effect and so did not legislate one into being. He did, however, try to introduce national testing into Scottish schools, but that policy was defeated because of a boycott by parents. Meanwhile the Scottish Consultative Council negotiated a 5–14 curriculum programme with teachers, parents and local authorities.

Bibliography

ABRAHAM, J. (1994) 'Positivism, structurationism and the differentiation-polarization theory: A reconsideration of Shilling's novelty and primacy thesis', *British Journal of Sociology of Education*, 15, 2, pp. 231–42.

ABRAHAM, J. and BIBBY, N. (1988) 'Mathematics and society: Ethnomathematics and a public educator curriculum', *For the Learning of Mathematics*, 8, 2, pp. 2–11.

ABRAHAM, J. and BIBBY, N. (1989) 'Human agency: The black box of mathematics in the curriculum', *Zentralblatt fur Didaktik der Mathermatik*, 5, pp. 183–8.

ACKER, J. (1973) 'Women and social stratification: A case of intellectual sexism', *American Journal of Sociology*, 78, pp. 936–45.

ACKER, S. (1981) 'No woman's land: British sociology of education 1960–1979', *Sociological Review*, 29, 1, pp. 79–104.

ACKER, S. (1983) 'Women and teaching: A semi-detached sociology of a semi-profession', in WALKER, S. and BARTON, L. (Eds) *Gender, Class and Education*, Basingstoke, Falmer Press.

AGGLETON, P.J. and WHITTY, G. (1985) 'Rebels without a cause? socialisation and subcultural style among the children of the new middle classes', *Sociology of Education*, 58, pp. 60–72.

ALLPORT, G.W. (1954) *The Nature of Prejudice*, Boston, MA, Addison-Wesley.

ANON (1986a) 'School sports ban "barmy"', *The Times*, 16 July.

ANON (1986b) 'Baker speaks up for the brightest', *Guardian*, 9 July.

ANON (1986c) 'Decline of school team spirit', *The Times*, 18 July.

ANON (1986d) 'Risk to pupils in the pursuit of equal treatment', *Guardian*, 30 July.

ANON (1994a) 'For council read quango', *Guardian*, 3 May.

ANON (1994b) 'Opting Out', *Guardian*, 24 May.

ANYON, J. (1981) 'Social class and school knowledge', *Curriculum Inquiry*, 1, 1, pp. 3–42.

ANYON, J. (1983) 'Intersections of gender and class: Accommodation and resistance by working class and affluent females to contradictory sex-role ideologies', in WALKER, S. and BARTON, L. (Eds) *Gender, Class and Education*, Sussex, Falmer Press.

APPLE, M. (1979) *Ideology and Curriculum*, London, Boston and Henley, Routledge and Kegan Paul.

BALL, S.J. (1981) *Beachside Comprehensive: A Case Study of Secondary Schooling*, London, Cambridge University Press.

BALL, S.J. (1984) (Ed) *Comprehensive Schooling: A Reader*, Sussex, Falmer Press.

BALL, S.J. (1993) 'Education markets, choice and social class: The market as a class strategy in the UK and the USA', *British Journal of Sociology of Education*, 14, 1, pp. 3–19.

BARNES, D. (1976) *From Communication to Curriculum*, Harmondsworth, Penguin Books.

BARTON, L. *et al.* (1980) *Schooling, Ideology and the Curriculum*, Sussex, Falmer Press.

BASH, L. and COULBY, D. (1989) *The Education Reform Act: Competition and Control*, London, Cassell.

BATES, R. (1980) 'New developments in the new sociology of education', *British Journal of Sociology of Education*, 1, 1, pp. 67–79.

BATES, S. (1990) 'Heads attack "competitive school acts"', *Guardian*, 30 May.

BATES, S. (1991) 'Geographers dismayed by Clarke's changes', *Guardian*, 15 January.

BECKETT, F. (1992) 'Going to business school', *Guardian*, 26 May.

BELLOS, A. (1993) 'Singled out by the state', *Guardian*, 26 October.

BENNETTO, J. (1993) 'Schools "forced to select pupils"', *Independent*, 14 March.

BENTLY, D. and WATTS, M. (1987) 'Courting the positive virtues: A case for feminist science', in KELLY, A. (Ed) *Science for Girls?* Milton Keynes, Open University Press.

BERLINER, W. (1991) 'Sweet streams?', *Guardian*, 12 November.

BERNSTEIN, B. (1971) 'On the classification and framing of educational knowledge', in YOUNG, M. (Ed) *Knowledge and Control: New Directions in the Sociology of Education*, London, Macmillan.

BERRILL, R. and WALLIS, P. (1976) 'Sex roles in mathematics', *Mathematics in School*, 5, 2, p. 28.

BHASKAR, R. (1975) *A Realist Theory of Science*, Sussex, Harvester Press.

BHASKAR, R. (1979) *The Possibility of Naturalism*, Sussex, Harvester.

BIBBY, N. (1983) 'Curricular Discontinuity', Unpublished M.A. Thesis, University of Sussex.

BLACKSTONE, T. (1976) 'The education of girls today', in MITCHELL, J. and OAKLEY, A. (Eds) *The Rights and Wrongs of Women*, Harmondsworth, Penguin Books.

BOURDIEU, P. (1973) 'Cultural reproduction and social reproduction', in BROWN, R. (Ed) *Knowledge, Education and Cultural Change*, London, Tavistock.

BOWE, R., BALL, S.J. and GOLD, A. (1992) *Reforming Education and Changing Schools*, London and New York, Routledge.

BOWLES, S. and GINTIS, H. (1976) *Schooling in Capitalist America: Education and the Contradictions of Economic Life*, London and Henley, Routledge and Kegan Paul.

BOYDE, F.C., COURT, R.A., COURT, A.M. and HAWDON, J.C. (1976) *Simple Modern Maths 1*, Nelson.

BRIGHOUSE, H. (1916) *Hobson's Choice*, London, Samuel French.

BROWN, R. (1973) *Knowledge, Education and Cultural Change*, London, Tavistock.

BURGESS, R.G. (1983) *Experiencing Comprehensive Education*, London and New York, Methuen.

BURTON, L. (1986) *Girls Into Maths Can Go*, London, Holt, Rinehart and Winston.

BURTON, L. and WEINER, G. (1990) 'Social justice and the National Curriculum', *Research Papers in Education*, 5, 3, pp. 203–27.

CENTRE FOR CONTEMPORARY CULTURAL STUDIES (1981) *Unpopular Education*, London, Hutchinson.

CICOURAL, A.V. and KITSUSE, J.I. (1963) *The Educational Decision-Makers*, New York, Bobbs Merrill.

CLIFFORD, P. and HEATH, A. (1984) 'Selection does make a difference', *Oxford Review of Education*, 10, 1, pp. 85–97.

COCKCROFT, W.H. (1982) *Mathematics Counts, Reports of the Committee of Inquiry into the Teaching of Mathematics in School*, London, HMSO.

CONNELL, R.W. (1983) *Which Way Is Up? Essays on Sex, Class and Culture*, Sydney, Allen and Unwin.

CORRIGAN, P. (1979) *Schooling the Smash Street Kids*, London, Macmillan.

COURT, R.A. and COURT, A.M. (1980) *Simple Modern Maths 3*, Surrey, Nelson.

CROALL, J. (1994) 'Class division', *Guardian*, 1 March.

CROMPTON, R. and SANDERSON, K. (1990) *Gendered Jobs and Social Change*, London, Unwin Hyman.

DALE, M. (1986) 'Stalking a conceptual chameleon: Ideology in marxist studies of education', *Educational Theory*, 36, 3, pp. 241–57.

DAVIES, L. (1983) 'Gender, resistance and power', in WALKER, S. and BARTON, L. (Eds) *Gender, Class and Education*, Sussex, Falmer Press.

DAVIES, L. (1984) *Pupil Power: Deviance and Gender in School*, Sussex, Falmer Press.

DAVIES, B. and ANDERSON, L. (1992) *Opting for Self-Management: The Early Experience of Grant-maintained Schools*, London, Routledge.

DAVIES, L. and MEIGHAN, R. (1975) 'A review of schooling and sex roles, with particular reference to the experience of girls in secondary schools', *Educational Review*, 27, pp. 165–78.

DEEM, R. (1978) *Women and Schooling*, London, Routledge and Kegan Paul.

DEEM, R. (Ed) (1980) *Schooling for Women's Work*, London, Routledge and Kegan Paul.

DELAMONT, S. (1970) *Sex Roles and the School*, London, Methuen.

DELAMONT, S. (1990) *Sex Roles and the School*, London, Routledge, 2nd ed.

DEMAINE, J. (1981) *Contemporary Theories in the Sociology of Education*, London and Basingstoke, Macmillan.

DENSCOMBE, M. (1982) 'The "Hidden Pedagogy" and its implications for teacher training', *British Journal of Sociology of Education*, 3, 2, pp. 249–65.

DEPARTMENT FOR EDUCATION (1994) *Our Children's Education: The Updated Parent's Charter*, London, DfE.

DICKENS, C. (1983) *Great Expectations*, Essex, Longman.

DOUGLAS, J.D. (1970) *The Relevance of Sociology*, New York, Appleton.

DOUGLAS, J.W.B. (1964) *The Home and the School*, London, MacGibbon and Kee.

DOUGLAS, J.W.B., ROSS, J.M. and SIMPSON, H.R. (1968) *All Our Future*, London, Peter Davies.

EASLEA, B. (1981) *Science and Sexual Oppression*, London, Weidenfeld and Nicolson.

ELLIOT, B. and MACLENNAN, D. (1994) 'Education, modernity and neo-conservative school reform in Canada, Britain and the USA', *British Journal of Sociology of Education*, 15, 2, pp. 165–86.

ENGLISH CENTRE (1986) *The English Curriculum*, Gender, Inner London Education Authority.

EVANS, T.D. (1982) 'Being and becoming: Teachers' perceptions of sex roles and their male and female pupils', *British Journal of Sociology of Education*, 3, 2, pp. 127–43.

FAIRHALL, J. (1988) 'Six out of 10 support ILEA', *Guardian*, 11 May.

FIELD, F. (1989) *Losing Out: The Emergence of Britain's Underclass*, Oxford, Blackwell.

FLANDERS, N. (1970) *Analysing Teacher Behaviour*, Reading, MA, Addison-Wesley.

FLOUD, J. and HALSEY, A.H. (1957) 'Social class, intelligence tests and selection for secondary schooling', *British Journal of Sociology*, 8, 1, pp. 33–9.

FLOUD, J., HALSEY, A.H. and MARTIN, F.M. (1966) *Social Class and Educational Opportunity*, Bath, Chivers.

FOGELMAN, K. (1984) 'Problems in comparing examination attainment in selective and comprehensive secondary schools', *Oxford Review of Education*, 10, 1, pp. 33–43.

FORD, J. (1969) *Social Class and the Comprehensive School*, London, Methuen.

FOUCAULT, M. (1979) *History of Sexuality*, London, Allen Lane, Penguin Books.

FRASIER, N. and SADKER, M. (1973) *Sexism in School and Society*, New York, Harper and Row.

FULLER, M. (1980) 'Black girls in a London comprehensive school', in DEEM, R. (Ed) *Schooling for Women's Work*, London, Routledge and Kegan Paul.

FURLONG, V.J. (1976) 'Interaction sets in the classroom', in STUBBS, M. and DELAMONT, S. (Eds) *Readings on Interaction in the Classroom*, London, Wiley.

FURLONG, V.J. (1984) 'Black resistance in the Liberal comprehensive', in DELAMONT, S. (Ed) *Readings on Interaction in the Classroom*, London, Methuen.

FURLONG, V.J. (1985) *The Deviant Pupil: Sociological Perspectives*, Milton Keynes, Open University Press.

GASKELL, J. (1985) 'Course enrollment in the high school: The perspective of working class females', *Sociology of Education*, 58, pp. 48–59.

GELSTHORPE, L. (1992) 'Response to Martyn Hammersley's paper "On Feminist Methodology"', *Sociology*, 26, 2, pp. 187–206.

GILBORN, D. (1994) 'The micro-politics of macro reform', *British Journal of Sociology of Education*, 15, 2, pp. 147–64.

GIROUX, H. (1983a) 'Theories of reproduction and resistance in the new sociology of education: A critical analysis', *Harvard Educational Review*, 53, 3, pp. 257–93.

GIROUX, H.A. (1983b) *Theory and Resistance in Education: A Pedagogy for the Opposition*, London, Heinemann Educational Books.

GLASS, D.V. (1954) *Social Mobility in Britain*, London, Routledge.

GOLDSTEIN, H. (1991) 'Secret of valued assessments', *Guardian*, 21 May.

GOLDSTEIN, H. and NUTTALL, D. (1989) 'Screen test for progress', *Guardian*, 27 July.

GOLDTHORPE, J.H. and PAYNE, C. (1986) 'Class mobility of women: Results from different approaches to the analysis of recent British data', *Sociology*, 20, 4, pp. 531–55.

GORBUTT, D. (1972) 'The new sociology of education', *Education for Teaching*, 89, pp. 3–9.

GOULDNER, A.W. (1970) 'Anti-minotaur: The myth of a value-free sociology', in DOUGLAS, J.D. (Ed) *The Relevance of Sociology*, New York, Appleton.

GOW, D. (1989) 'Key to pupil success "lies in school rather than race"', *Guardian*, 28 June.

GRAFTON, T., MILLER, H., SMITH, L., VEGODA, M. and WHITFIELD, R. (1983) 'Gender and curriculum choice: A case study', in HAMMERSLEY, M. and HARGREAVES, A. (Eds) *Curriculum Practice*, London, Falmer Press.

GRAY, J., MCPHERSON, A.F. and RAFFE, D. (1983) *Reconstructions of Secondary Education*, London, Routledge and Kegan Paul.

GRAY, J., JESSON, D. and JONES, B. (1984) 'Predicting differences in examination results between local education authorities: Does school organisation matter?', *Oxford Review of Education*, 10, 1, pp. 45–68.

GREGSON, N. and LOWE, M. (1994) 'Waged domestic labour and the renegotiation of the domestic division of labour within dual career households', *Sociology*, 28, 1, pp. 55–78.

GRONLUND, N.E. (1959) *Sociometry in the Classroom*, New York, Harper and Row.

HAMMERSLEY, M. and ATKINSON, P. (1983) *Ethnography: Principles in Practice*, London and New York, Tavistock.

HAMMERSLEY, M. (1985) 'From ethnography to theory: A programme and paradigm in the sociology of education', *Sociology*, 19, 2, pp. 244–59.

HARGREAVES, A. (1982) 'Resistance and relative autonomy theories: Problems of distortion in recent Marxist analyses of education', *British Journal of Sociology of Education*, 3, 2, pp. 107–26.

HARGREAVES, D.H. (1967) *Social Relations in a Secondary School*, London and Henley, Routledge and Kegan Paul.

HARGREAVES, D.H. (1982) *The Challenge for the Comprehensive School*, London, Routledge and Kegan Paul.

HARTLEY, D. (1980) 'Sex differences in the infant school: Definitions and theories', *British Journal of the Sociology of Education*, 1, 1, pp. 93–105.

HEATH, A. (1984) 'In defence of comprehensive schools', *Oxford Review of Education*, 10, 1, pp. 115–23.

HERZOG, A.R. (1982) 'High school seniors' occupational plans and values: Trends in sex differences 1976 through 1980', *Sociology of Education*, 55, pp. 1–13.

HMSO (1975) *A Language for Life* (Bullock Report).

HOGBEN, L. (1938) *Political Arithmetic: A Symposium of Population Studies*, London, Allen and Unwin.

HOLLY, D.N. (1965) 'Profiting from a comprehensive school: Class, sex and ability', *British Journal of Sociology*, 16, 4, pp. 150–58.

HUMPHRIES, S. (1981) *Hooligans or Rebels?*, Oxford, Basil Blackwell.

JACKSON, B. and MARSDEN, D. (1962) *Education and the Working Class*, London, Routledge and Kegan Paul.

JOHNSON, R. (1979) '"Really useful knowledge": Radical education and working class culture', in CLARKE, J., CRITCHER, C. and JOHNSON, R. (Eds) *Working Class Culture*, London, Hutchinson.

JUDD, J. (1990) 'On to the fast track or into the rat race?', *Sunday Independent*, 25 February.

JUDD, J. (1993) 'Teachers to boycott national testing', *Independent*, 10 March.

JUDD, J. and STRICKLAND, S. (1993) 'Illiterate England', *Independent on Sunday*, 7 February.

KANER, P. (1985) *Integrated Mathematics Scheme, M2*, London, Bell and Hyman.

KEAT, R. (1981) *The Politics of Social Theory*, Oxford, Basil Blackwell.

KEDDIE, N. (1971) 'Classroom knowledge', in YOUNG, M. (Ed) *Knowledge and Control: New Directions in the Sociology of Education*, London, Macmillan.

KELLY, A. (1981) *The Missing Half*, Manchester, Manchester University Press.

KELLY, A. (1985) 'The construction of masculine science', *British Journal of the Sociology of Education*, 6, 2, pp. 133–54.

KENWAY, J. *et al.* (1994) 'Making "Hope Practical" rather than "Despair Convincing": Feminist post-structuralism, gender reform and educational change', *British Journal of Sociology of Education*, 15, 2, pp. 187–210.

KESSLER, S., ASHENDEN, D.J., CONNELL, R.W. and DOWSETT, G.W. (1985) 'Gender relations in secondary schooling', *Sociology of Education*, 58, pp. 34–48.

KING, R. (1987) 'Sex and social class inequalities in education: A re-examination', *British Journal of Sociology of Education*, 8, pp. 287–303.

LABOV, W. (1972) *Language in the Inner City*, University of Pennsylvania.

LACEY, C. (1966) 'Some sociological concomitants of academic streaming in a grammar school', *British Journal of Sociology*, 17, 3, pp. 245–62.

LACEY, C. (1970) *Hightown Grammar*, Manchester, Manchester University Press.

LACEY, C. (1977) *The Socialisation of Teachers*, London, Methuen.

LAMBART, A. (1976) 'The sisterhood', in HAMMERSLEY, M. and WOODS, P. (Eds) *The Process of Schooling*, London and Henley, Routledge and Kegan Paul.

LAWSON, J. and SILVER, H. (1973) *A Social History of Education in England*, London, Methuen.

LEE, C. (1983) *The Ostrich Position: Sex, Schooling and Mystification*, London, Unwin.

LEES, S. (1986) *Losing Out: Sexuality and Adolescent Girls*, London, Hutchinson.

LEES, S. (1993) *Sugar and Spice: Sexuality and Adolescent Girls*, Harmondsworth, Penguin Books.

LOBBAN, G. (1975) 'Sex-roles in reading schemes', *Educational Review*, 27, pp. 202–10.

LORTIE, D.C. (1975) *Schoolteachers: A Sociological Study*, Chicago, University of Chicago Press.

LUEPTOW, L.B. (1981) 'Sex-typing and change in the occupational choices of high school seniors: 1964–1975', *Sociology of Education*, 54, pp. 16–24.

LUKES, S. (1973) 'On the social determination of truth', in HORTON, R. and FINNEGAN, R. (Eds) *Modes of Thought*, London, Faber.

MAC AN GHAILL, M. (1988) *Young, Gifted and Black: Student–teacher Relations in the Schooling of Black Youth*, Milton Keynes, Open University Press.

MACDONALD, M. (1980) 'Sociocultural reproduction and women's education', in DEEM, R. (Ed) *Schooling For Women's Work*, London, Routledge and Kegan Paul.

MACLEOD, D. (1993) 'Schools have £400 million in bank "as teachers are sacked"', *Guardian*, 15 July.

MACLEOD, D. (1994) 'Uniformity of choice', *Guardian*, 17 May.

MAHONEY, P. (1985) *Schools for the Boys?*, London, Hutchinson.

MANN, K. (1992) *The Making of an English 'Underclass'?*, Milton Keynes, Open University Press.

MARKS, J., COX, C. and POMIAN-SRZADNICKI, M. (1983) *Standards in English Schools*, London, National Council for Educational Standards.

MARSHALL, J. (1983) 'Developing anti-sexist initiatives in education', *International Journal of Political Education*, 6, pp. 113–37.

MARTYNA, W. (1980) 'Beyond the "He/Man" approach: The case for non-sexist language', *Signs: Journal of Women in Culture and Society*, 5, 3, pp. 482–93.

MCPHERSON, A. and WILLMS, J.D. (1987) 'Equalization and improvement: Some effects of comprehensive reorganization in Scotland', *Sociology*, 21, 4, pp. 509–39.

MCROBBIE, A. (1978) 'Working class girls and the culture of femininity', in WOMEN'S STUDY GROUP CENTRE FOR CONTEMPORARY CULTURAL STUDIES (Eds) *Women Take Issue*, London, Hutchinson.

MCROBBIE, A. and NOVA, M. (1982) *Gender and Generation*, London, Macmillan.

MEASOR, L. (1983) 'Gender and the sciences: Pupils' gender-based conceptions of school subjects', in HAMMERSLEY, M. and HARGREAVES, A. (Eds) *Curriculum Practice*, London, Falmer Press.

MEIKLE, J. (1990) 'Facts "hold key" to history teaching', *Guardian*, 29 December.

MEIKLE, J. (1993) 'Opt-out schools suffer budget cuts in government "clawback"', *Guardian*, 27 July.

MEIKLE, J. (1994a) 'Curriculum battle heads for truce', *Guardian*, 4 January.

MEIKLE, J. (1994b) 'Not voting with their feet', *Guardian*, 18 January.

MEIKLE, J. (1994c) 'Tables are turning', *Guardian*, 7 June.

MEYENN, R. (1980) 'School girls' peer groups', in WOODS, P. (Ed) *Pupil Strategies: Explorations in the Sociology of the School*, London, Croom Helm.

MICKELSON, R.A. (1980) 'Social stratification processes in secondary schools: A comparison of Beverly Hills high school and Morningside high school', *Journal of Education*, 167, 4, pp. 83–112.

MONTEITH, M. (1979) 'Boys, girls and language', *English In Education*, 13, 2, pp. 3–6.

MOORE, S., ANTROBUS, A.L. and PUGH, G.F. (1978) *Longman Audio-Visual French Stage A4*, (New impression, First published 1969), Longman.

MOORE, S., ANTROBUS, A.L. and PUGH, G.F. (1982) *Longman Audio-Visual French Stage A3*, (Fourteenth impression, First published in 1968), Longman.

MOORE, S., ANTROBUS, A.L., PUGH, G.F., GREEN, M.G.A. and OETERS, W. (1982) *Longman Audio-Visual French Stage B3*, (Twelfth impression, First published in 1969), Longman.

MOORE, S., ANTROBUS, A.L., PUGH, G.F. and JANNETTA, G.A. (1977) *Longman Audio-Visual French Stage B4*, (Sixth impression, First published 1970), Longman.

NATRIELLO, G. and McDILL, E.L. (1986) 'Performance standards, student effort on homework, and academic achievement', *Sociology of Education*, 59, pp. 18–31.

NORTHAM, J. (1982) 'Girls and boys in primary maths books', *Education*, 10, 1, pp. 11–14.

OFFICE OF POPULATION AND CENSUSES AND SURVEYS (1980) *Classification of Occupations*, London, Her Majesty's Stationery Office.

PAYNE, J. and PAYNE, C. (1994) 'Recession, restructuring and the fate of the unemployed: Empirical evidence in the underclass debate', *Sociology*, 28, 1, pp. 1–19.

PEDLEY, R. (1969) *The Comprehensive School*, Harmondsworth, Penguin Books.

PETTY, M.F. and HOGBEN, D. (1980) 'Explorations of semantic space with beginning teachers: A study of socialisation into teaching', *British Journal of Teacher Education*, 6, pp. 51–61.

PHILLIPS, M. (1993) 'The head of the family', *Guardian*, 23 February.

PRATT, J., BLOOMFIELD, J. and SEALE, C. (1984) *Option Choice: A Question of Equal Opportunity*, Windsor, National Foundation for Educational Research-Nelson.

PRING, R. (1972) 'Knowledge out of Control', *Education for Teaching*, 89, pp. 19–28.

QUINE, W.G. (1974) 'Polarised cultures in comprehensive schools', *Research in Education*, 12, pp. 9–25.

RATTIGAN, T. (1953) 'The Winslow boy', in RATTIGAN, T. (Ed) *The Collected Plays of Terence Rattigan*, London, Hamish Hamilton.

REYNOLDS, D., SULLIVAN, M. and MURGATROYD, S. (1987) *The Comprehensive Experiment*, London, Falmer Press.

RIDDELL, S. (1992) *Gender and the Politics of the Curriculum*, London, Routledge.

ROBERTSON, J. (1981) *Effective Classroom Control*, London, Hodder and Stoughton.

ROYAL SOCIETY AND INSTITUTE OF MATHEMATICS AND ITS APPLICATIONS (1986) *Girls and Mathematics*, The Royal Society.

SAPIR, E. (1970) *Culture, Language and Personality: Selected Essays* (edited by MANDELBAUM, D.G.) California, University of California Press.

SARTRE, J.P. (1957) *Being and Nothingness*, London, Methuen.

SARUP, M. (1978) *Marxism and Education*, London, Routledge and Kegan Paul.

SAUNDERS, P. (1990) *A Nation of Home Owners*, London, Unwin Hyman.

SCHOOLS COUNCIL (1973) *The Never Not Nothing No More Book*, Leeds, Arnold.

SCHUTZ, A. (1967) *The Phenomenology of the Social World*, Northwestern University Press.

SHAKESPEARE, W. (1984) 'Julius Caesar', in HUMPHREYS, A. (Ed) *The Oxford Shakespeare: Julius Caesar*, Oxford and New York, Oxford University Press.

SHARP, R. (1980) *Knowledge, Ideology and the Politics of Schooling*, London, Routledge.

SHARP, R. and GREEN, A. (1975) *Education and Social Control*, London and Boston, Routledge and Kegan Paul.

SHAW, J. (1980) 'Education and the individual: Schooling for girls or mixed schooling a mixed blessing?' in DEEM, R. (Ed) *Schooling for Women's Work*, London, Routledge and Kegan Paul.

SHILLING, C. (1992) 'Reconceptualising structure and agency in the sociology of education: Structuration theory and schooling', *British Journal of Sociology of Education*, 13, pp. 69–87.

SHIPMAN, M. (Ed) (1975) *The Organisation and Impact of Social Research*, London, Routledge and Kegan Paul.

SMART, C. and SMART, B. (1978) *Women, Sexuality and Social Control*, London, Routledge and Kegan Paul.

SOFER, A. (1986) 'Sporting chances', *The Times Educational Supplement*, 18 July.

SPENDER, D. (1978) 'The facts of life: Sex differentiated knowledge in the English classroom and the school', *English in Education*, 12, 3, pp. 1–9.

SPENDER, D. (1980) *Man Made Language*, London, Boston and Henley, Routledge and Kegan Paul.

SPENDER, D. (1980) 'Talking in class', in SPENDER, D. and SARAH, E. (Eds) *Learning to Lose*, London, Women's Press, 1st Ed.

SPENDER, D. and SARAH, E. (Eds) (1988) *Learning to Lose; Sexism and Education*, London, Women's Press, 2nd Ed.

STANLEY, J. (1986) 'Sex and the quiet schoolgirl', *British Journal of Sociology of Education*, 7, pp. 275–86.

STANWORTH, M. (1981) *Gender and schooling: A Study of Sexual Divisions in the Classroom*, London, Hutchinson.

STEEDMAN, J. (1983) *Examination Results in Selective and Non-selective Secondary Schools*, London, National Children's Bureau.

STEVENS, A. (1980) *Clever Children in Comprehensive Schools*, Harmondsworth, Penguin.

STRAWSON, P. (1970) *Meaning and Truth*, Oxford, Oxford University Press.

STUBBS, M. and DELAMONT, S. (1976) *Explorations in Classroom Observation*, Chichester, Wiley and Sons.

SWEETMAN, J. (1993) 'Higher thoughts on teacher training', *Guardian*, 19 October.

SWEETMAN, J. (1994a) 'Unwrapping Sir Ron's christmas parcel', *Guardian*, 11 January.

SWEETMAN, J. (1994b) 'Hard times ahead for the juggernaut jugglers', *Guardian*, 18 January.

TAYLOR, J. (1979) 'Sexist bias in physics textbooks', *Physics Education*, 14, pp. 227–80.

THOMAS, D. (1954) *Under Milk Wood*, London, Dent.

THORNDIKE, R.L. and HAGEN, E. (1973a) *Cognitive Abilities Test Levels A–H, Junior School and Secondary School: Teacher's Book-Procedures*, London, Thomas Nelson and Sons.

THORNDIKE, R.L. and HAGEN, E. (1973b) *Cognitive Abilities Test Levels A–H, Junior School and Secondary School*, London, Thomas Nelson and Sons.

THORNDIKE, R.L. and HAGEN, E. (1973c) *Cognitive Abilities Test Levels A–H, Junior School and Secondary School: Tables of Norms and Their Interpretation*, London, Thomas Nelson and Sons.

TRENCHARD, L. (1988) 'Young lesbians in school', in SPENDER, D. and SARAH, E. (Eds) *Learning to Lose: Sexism and Education*, London, Women's Press, 2nd Ed, pp. 193–200.

TYTLER, D. (1994) 'Spoilt choice', *Guardian*, 1 March.

VAUGHAN, C. (1990) 'Unbalanced laughter', *Guardian*, 27 March.

WALFORD, G. (1980) 'Sex bias in physics textbooks', *School Science Review*, pp. 220–27.

WALFORD, G. (1981) 'Do chemistry textbooks present a sex biased image', *Education In Chemistry*, 18, pp. 18–19.

WALKER, J.C. (1985) 'Rebels with our applause? A critique of resistance theory in Paul Willis's ethnography of schooling', *Journal of Education*, 167, 2, pp. 63–83.

WALKER, J.C. (1986) 'Romanticising resistance, romanticising culture: Problems in Willis's theory of cultural production', *British Journal of Sociology of Education*, 7, 1, pp. 59–80.

WARD, D. (1991) 'Drive that the teachers' MoT creates', *Guardian*, 14 May.

WEINER, G. (1980) 'Sex differences in mathematical performance: A review of research and possible action', in DEEM, R. (Ed) *Schooling for Women's Work*, London, Routledge and Kegan Paul.

WESTERGAARD, J. (1992) 'About and beyond the "Underclass": Some notes on influences of social climate on British sociology today', *Sociology*, 26, 4, pp. 575–88.

WESTON, C. (1989a) 'Streaming prospect for primary schools', *Guardian*, 14 April.

WESTON, C. (1989b) 'Baker defeated on grammar', *Guardian*, 23 June.

WESTON, C. (1990) 'Home life is key to top marks at school', *Guardian*, 9 March.

WEXLER, P. (1982) 'Structure, text and subject: A critical sociology of school knowledge', in APPLE, M.W. (Ed) *Cultural and Economic Reproduction in Education: Essays on Class, Ideology and the State*, London, Routledge and Kegan Paul.

WHEELOCK, J. (1990) *Husbands at Home: The Domestic Economy in a Post-Industrial Society*, London, Routledge.

WHITE, J. (1988) 'An unconstitutional national curriculum', in LAWTON, D. and CHITTY, C. (Eds) *The National Curriculum*, London, Institute of Education.

WHITTY, G. (1985) *Sociology and School Knowledge*, London, Methuen.

WHORF, B.L. (1956) 'Language, thought and reality: Essays of Benjamin Whorf', in CARROL, J.B. (Ed) Cambridge, MA, MIT Press.

WHYLD, J. (1983) (Ed) *Sexism in the Secondary Curriculum*, London, Harper and Row.

WILLIAMS, A. (1993) 'Diversity and agreement in feminist ethnography', *Sociology*, 27, 4, pp. 575–90.

WILLIS, P. (1977) *Learning to Labour: How Working Class Kids Get Working Class Jobs*, England, Saxon House.

WILLIS, P. (1981) 'Cultural production is different from cultural reproduction is different from social reproduction is different from reproduction', *Interchange*, 12, 2–3, pp. 48–67.

WITKIN, R.W. (1974) 'Social class influence on the amount and type of positive evaluation of school lessons', in EGGLESTON, S.J. (Ed) *Contemporary Research in the Sociology of Education*, London, Methuen.

WITTGENSTEIN, L. (1963) *Philosophical Investigations*, Oxford, Basil Blackwell.

WOOD, J. (1984) 'Groping towards sexism: Boys' sex talk', in MCROBBIE, A. and NOVA, M. (Eds) *Gender and Generation*, London, Macmillan.

WOODS, P. (1979) *The Divided School*, London, Routledge and Kegan Paul.

WOODS, P. (1980) (Ed) *Pupil Strategies*, London, Croom Helm.

WOOLGAR, S. (1988) (Ed) *Knowledge and Reflexivity*, London, Sage.

WRIGHT, E. (1982) '"He" or "She" in use: Assumptions about writing', *English in Education*, 16, 3.

WRIGHTMILLS, C. (1959) *The Sociological Imagination*, Oxford, OUP.

YATES, P. (1980) *Immigration and Education: A Study of an Asian Community and a Comprehensive School*, University of Sussex, D.Phil Thesis.

YOUNG, M.F.D. (1971) (Ed) *Knowledge and Control: New Directions for the Sociology of Education*, London, Macmillan.

YOUNG, M.F.D. (1973) 'Taking sides against the probable: Problems of relativism and commitment in teaching and the sociology of knowledge', *Educational Review*, 25, 3, pp. 210–22.

Index